HIS
TRUTH

HIS
TRUTH

Scriptural Truths About Basic Doctrines

JACK COTTRELL

College Press Publishing Company, Joplin, Missouri

Library of Congress Catalog Card Number: 79-67437
International Standard Book Number: 0-89900-328-1

CONTENTS

CHAPTER ONE

Truth About
Scripture

Suppose you had never seen a Bible, or known anyone who had. What kind of God would you be worshiping just now? Would you be worshiping a sacred tree, or a snake, or "the Force"? What would you believe about where the human race came from and where it is going? Would you perhaps think of the physical body as a kind of punishment for spirits who sinned? Would you then think of salvation as escaping from bodily existence?

Would there be any way at all to answer such questions? Would there be any source of *truth* about God and Man?

The answer is yes. Even if there were no Bible, man would not be entirely lacking in such knowledge. The created universe itself reveals to us certain things about God and His relationship to man. The revelation that comes through nature is sometimes called *general* revelation, because it is available to everyone in general and because the truth known thereby is general rather than specific.

For instance, the immensity and orderliness of the universe tell us that its Maker is full of power and wisdom and is worthy to be praised (Psa. 19:1). The earth's natural bounty testifies to the essential goodness of the Creator (Matt. 5:45; Acts 14:17). The creation is so marvelous in every way that it is obviously the product of an all-powerful being who alone is God (Rom. 1:18-20).

Corresponding to this knowledge of God as Creator is a knowledge of our general responsibilities as creatures who are completely dependent upon Him. We know, for instance, that we should honor the Creator as God, and thank Him for His bounty (Rom. 1:21,22). There also seems to be a kind of built-in knowledge of basic moral principles (Rom. 2:14,15), probably as the result of our being made in God's image.

The point is that these truths are not just knowable, but are actually known ("clearly seen," Rom. 1:20), through general revelation alone.

Now the critical question is this: how has this truth been treated by those having general revelation only (usually called "the heathen")? Romans 1:18-32 gives the distressing answer: it has been suppressed, corrupted, and distorted. True and simple worship has been replaced by idolatry of the worst kind. The rankest sin is heartily practiced in conscious recognition of its perversity, and God's wrath is justly directed against such sinners, since their knowledge makes them without excuse.

Remember: all this is true even where there is no Biblical revelation, where only general revelation is available. Thus Paul can say that *all* have sinned and are guilty before God

SCRIPTURE

(Rom. 3:9-20).

Here we reach the limits of general revelation. It tells us about God as Creator; it makes us aware of law and sin. But it can never show us God as Savior; through it we could never learn of grace and salvation. This is the dilemma of man under general revelation alone: he inescapably knows enough to be lost, but can never know enough to be saved. This latter knowledge can come only through the special revelation that focuses on the Savior, Jesus Christ (Rom. 10:13-17).

In summary, the sinner's ultimate need is for salvation, but his most immediate need is for truth. The truth given through general revelation he has denied or distorted; truth about salvation is not even available by this means. Thus sinful man needs more than general revelation. He needs specially-revealed truth about God, man, sin, and salvation — truth that is uncorrupted, clear, and complete. This is what the Bible is all about. God's word is truth, the truth that shall make us free (John 17:17; 8:32).

The remainder of this chapter will focus on the nature of the Bible as an essential part of God's plan of salvation. The Bible is truth from God, truth for sinners, and truth forever sure.

TRUTH FROM GOD

A famous philosopher once said that if he had to choose between the search for truth and the possession of truth, he would choose the former. Such a choice betrays a very shallow understanding of man's present condition. When facing destruction one desperately needs to know the whole truth (1) about his predicament and (2) about the way out of it. There

9

is no time for a leisurely search. We need truth, and we need it now.

For instance, if a person is stricken with a high fever, pain and swelling in the chest and abdomen, and a rapidly falling blood count, he needs to know his problem's cause and cure fast. Mankind's spiritual problem is infinitely more serious than this, and the need for truth is correspondingly greater.

God Alone Is the Sure Source of Truth

Where can we find this truth? Is it possible that man may discover it himself? Not really. Despite our pretensions, we must admit that man is not a reliable source of truth. The reason is twofold.

First, our *intellects* are finite or limited. Using reason alone, we can never be certain we have discerned the truth about any subject. Even our five senses can be deceived; we do not always "see" what we think we see. Our senses are like filters through which all data from outside our minds must pass. We can never know for sure what has been filtered out and what has been able to come through without being changed in some way. For instance, is the orangeness that actually exists in an orange identical with the bright color I perceive in my mind?

If there is a degree of uncertainty even with regard to things knowable through our senses, we are even less competent to learn the truth about abstract concepts. If I can't be sure about the color of an orange, I must be even less sure of the truth about justice or man's purpose or eternal life.

Second, our *wills* prevent us from depending on ourselves as a reliable source of truth. Even the truth we do have is likely to be suppressed or distorted because of sin, as Romans 1 indicates.

Thus, if we really want to know the truth about our prob-lem and its solution, we must turn to God. God alone is the sure source of truth. He is all-knowing, all-wise, and all-good. His knowledge is perfect and His word is truth (John 17:17).

The Bible Is from God

That God is a sure source of truth benefits us only if He decides to communicate with us. But has He? Yes! We can rejoice that God has chosen to speak with mankind, and He has done so in a way more precise and direct than the general revelation that comes through creation. He has addressed us with words; He has spoken to us in human language. And He has left His message with us in a permanent form, namely, the Bible.

Some parts of the Bible are direct revelations from God, even though they were written down by men. Examples of this are the Ten Commandments, the law of Moses in general, and the Sermon on the Mount.

Other parts of the Bible are the recollections and reflec-tions of men. For instance, when the apostle John tells of his and Peter's race to the empty tomb, he is not receiving a reve-lation but is remembering something from his own experience (John 20:1-8). David's psalm of repentance (Psa. 51) and Paul's assurance to the Romans that he truly wants to visit them (Rom. 1 :10-15) represent the sincere thoughts and feel-ings of their own hearts.

Some have the mistaken idea that only the parts of the Bible that are directly revealed can be considered truth from God. This is not so, however. God's participation in the pro-duction of the Bible includes not only revelation but also inspiration, which is the Holy Spirit's supervision of the writ-ing of all parts of the Bible: revelations, recollections, and

11

reflections. This means that God is directly involved in the authorship or origin of every word in Scripture.

This is what II Timothy 3:16 tells us: "All Scripture is inspired by God." The word *inspired* literally means "God-breathed," or "breathed out by God." Thus all Scripture is the result of divine activity. In some cases the out-breathing of Scripture included direct revelation, as in the case of prophecies regarding the future (Psa. 22:11-21; Micah 5:2). In other cases the out-breathing by God involved a stimulation of the human author's memory, guaranteeing its adequacy and accuracy (John 14:26). At other times the out-breathing was no more than a close supervision of the writer's reflections. But God stands behind every word of Scripture as its ultimate author.

Other references to the divine origin of Scripture include John 16:12-15; II Peter 1:20,21; Matthew 1:22; Luke 1:70; and II Samuel 23:2.

The Bible Is Truth

Because the Bible is inspired by God, it is completely true. Indeed, this is one of the main purposes of inspiration: to guarantee the truth of the product. Jesus promised to give His apostles the Spirit of truth, so that He could guide them into all truth (John 16:13). Whatever is God's word is necessarily true (John 17:17). Jesus declares that "Scripture cannot be broken" (John 10:35).

Sometimes the Bible is described as being inerrant or without error. This applies to every part of Scripture: its revelations, its recollections, its reflections. Strictly speaking it applies only to the original writings, not to copies and translations. The latter are usually accurate, though, and can be checked against a carefully-determined reconstruction of the originals.

12

TRUTH FOR SINNERS

The Bible is indeed truth from God. This does not mean that it contains all possible truth about all possible subjects. This is not God's intention. Its basic purpose is to show us the truth about the relationship between God and mankind. Thus we do not expect the Bible to give us details about nuclear physics or raising strawberries.

Something else that determines the scope and message of the Bible is the fact that it has been designed for sinners. Its message is a message that sinners need to know: truth about God, about man, about sin, about salvation.

The Bible's basic message to sinners is twofold. First there is *law*, usually in the form of *commandments*. Through the laws of the Bible a sinner becomes conscious of his sin (Rom. 3:20; 7:7). That is to say, he learns what sin is, and he is forced to face the truth that he is a sinner.

Knowing ourselves as sinners forces us to see our need for salvation. Thus the law prepares us for and drives us to the Savior (see Gal. 3:24). It lays the necessary foundation for the second part of the Bible's message to sinners, namely, the *gospel* (in the form of *promises.*)

The gospel of salvation is the main theme of the Bible, the central truth in the total world view presented therein. It is designed to show sinners how to be saved. Salvation by grace through the blood of Christ is the "scarlet thread" that runs throughout the Bible. This is its basic truth, the truth that sets sinners free (John 8:32).

Since the Bible is truth for sinners, it addresses us as we are, namely, as sinners. The Bible's basic message is one that even sinners can understand if they approach it honestly and objectively (Rom. 1:16; 10:13-17; Heb. 4:12).

TRUTH FOREVER SURE

This is a time when relativism and subjectivism reign supreme. It is widely believed that there is no such thing as absolute truth; nothing is always true or always false. Thus one can accept whatever "truths" appeal to him at the moment.

To some people this may sound like a very convenient arrangement, but to many others it is a source of despair. To be lost without knowing the way out; to face death without knowing how to escape its sting; to sense the certainty of judgment without knowing forgiveness — could anything be more agonizing? And the pain is only slightly relieved when the only solutions we have are subjective opinions and the relative conclusions of the moment.

This is why it is such an indescribable blessing to have the Bible as our source of truth. It is like a solid rock in the midst of quicksand. It is a firm foundation for hope and trust and assurance.

Its truth is *absolute*. It abides forever; it does not change. When Jesus says that "Scripture cannot be broken" (John 10:35), He is telling us that we can always count on God's Word. It never fails. It is truth forever sure. As Jesus puts it, "Heaven and earth will pass away, but My words shall not pass away" (Matt. 24:35). "The word of the Lord abides forever," says I Peter 1:25 (quoting Isa. 40:8). Even if every other word in the universe fails, God's Word will still be true (Rom. 3:4).

Its truth is *objective*. It is openly available to everyone in the same way. It is not a will-o'-the-wisp that one can perceive only with a special insight. We can know God's message without having to depend upon our own inner feelings

14

and hasty opinions.

Its truth is *authoritative*. Because the Bible is absolute and objective truth from God, we must submit our minds, our wills, our whole lives to it. It must be our only sure rule of faith. That is to say, our doctrines (what we believe and teach) must be drawn from God's written Word. Also, it must be our only sure rule of practice: that is, our ideas about right and wrong must be based upon the Bible.

Some think that submission to Scripture is a burden, a state of bondage. But truth does not enslave; it liberates. This is the promise to all who yield to Biblical authority: "You shall know the truth, and the truth shall make you free" (John 8:32).

CHAPTER TWO

Truth About
God
Creator and Ruler

It is presumptuous to try to present all the Biblical teach-ings about God in such a brief space as this. What is included here, then, can be regarded as no more than an overall outline of the more essential material.

We can best understand who God is in terms of his three major works: creation, providence, and redemption. For instance, when we know what it means to say that God is Cre-ator, we will be better able to understand certain aspects of His nature. The same is true of His other works.

GOD IS CREATOR

Thus we begin with a discussion of creation, which has

been defined as "that free act of God by which in the beginning He made, without the use of preexisting materials, the whole visible and invisible universe" (Crawford).

To say that creation is a "free act" means that He did not have to create anything; He was not compelled to do so by loneliness or love. It was a free decision: God created simply because He wanted to (Rev. 4:11).

The "invisible universe" is the world of spiritual beings, namely, the angels. This includes both the righteous angels and the angels who sinned (II Pet. 2:4), becoming the devil and demons. These are all created beings, including Satan himself.

The most significant element in the creation is the fact that everything was made "without the use of preexisting materials." This is sometimes referred to as creation *ex nihilo*, "from nothing." Before God began to create, nothing existed except God himself. By an act of sheer creative power God brought both matter and created spirits into existence.

The fact of creation is a primary teaching of Scripture. Genesis 1:1 says, "In the beginning God created the heavens and the earth." Hebrews 11:3 suggests the *ex nihilo* idea: "By faith we understand that the worlds were prepared by the word of God, so that what is seen was not made out of things which are visible." The eternal Logos (who became Jesus of Nazareth) was active in the creation: "All things came into being through Him" (John 1:3). See also Psalm 33:6; Colossians 1:16; Romans 4:17.

It should be noted that the Biblical doctrine of creation is unique, particularly the concept of creation from nothing. No other concept of the origin of the universe is like it. Consequently no other concept of God is like the Biblical one.

The Nature of the Creator

What is the nature of the God who "calls into being that which does not exist"? (Rom. 4:17). What attributes must such a God possess? (Let us note this point: what is true of God the Father is also true of God the Son and God the Holy Spirit.)

He is definitely transcendent. This means that He is *different* from created being, *other* than creation or *beyond* it. He alone is uncreated Spirit; every other being has been created. The very essence of God is thus different in kind from that of creatures. The distinction between Creator and creature is basic (Rom. 1:25; 1 Tim. 6:16).

The basic difference is that the transcendent God is infinite, which means unlimited. He is unlimited regarding time: He is eternal. This means He has no beginning and no ending. It also means He is above time and sees the whole sweep of time from beginning to end in a single glance. See Psalm 102:25-27; Isaiah 44:6; 46:9,10; Revelation 1:8.

God is also unlimited regarding space: He is omnipresent or everywhere-present at the same time. He is completely present and consciously active in every part of space at all times. See Psalm 139:7-10.

God is also unlimited regarding power: He is omnipotent or almighty. Certainly if God can create this vast universe from nothing, He can do anything He wants to do. See Revelation 1:8; Psalm 115:3; Matthew 19:26.

Because God is transcendent and thus unlimited in so many ways, He is understandably incomprehensible to us finite creatures. This means that we cannot really understand what God's nature is like. The knowledge we have is true and accurate, but it cannot be complete. The finite cannot completely grasp the infinite. See Deuteronomy 29:29; Isaiah 40:18,28; Romans 11:33.

Implications for Creatures

The fact of creation is one of the most important Biblical teachings. When this fact is ignored or denied, all kinds of errors and false doctrines arise. On the other hand, an understanding of this fact is the key to many of the problems of philosophy, ethics, and theology. Here we can list only a few of the more important implications.

1. Creation means that this physical universe — physical matter — is inherently good. God created it and pronounced it "very good" (Gen. 1:31). Any corruption that exists in the universe (e.g., disease and human death) is not natural and inherent but is the result of sin. See Romans 8:19-23. (Many religious philosophies have considered matter to be inherently evil, which results in all kinds of other errors and distortions.)

2. Creation supplies this universe and its history with a purpose and a goal. Here is the answer to the most urgent philosophical problem: what is the meaning of it all? Any philosophy that rules out creation can never answer this question. Only a deliberate act of creation by a personal God makes a purpose and a goal possible. Otherwise the universe is meaningless and absurd: it's just there.

3. Creation gives human life purpose and meaning. What is true of the universe as a whole is also true of its parts. If God did not create human life, then it has no meaning. The question, "What does it mean to be human?" has no answer. Or rather, it has as many answers as we want to give it, with none being any more "right" than the others.

4. Creation provides a basis for morality. Only a transcendent Creator-God has the ability to set absolute rules and

standards for right and wrong. Otherwise all norms are relative, and the concept of sin is meaningless. Also, only a transcendent Creator-God has the kind of inherent authority that absolutely obligates us to obey these rules.

5. Creation means that we are forever creatures, that we are not now and never will be divine in any sense. The human soul is not a little piece of God. Salvation never involves becoming divine or becoming gods, as many false religions teach (e.g., Mormonism, Armstrongism).

6. Creation requires that we also stand in awe of the Creator. It is the foundation for worship. We must always regard God with the fear of reverence.

7. Creation is the basis for stewardship responsibilities. God owns everything by right of creation; we are only stewards of the things we possess. This has implications for ecology, too.

It is well known that the modern world has all but abandoned the concept of creation. Is it any wonder that there is such chaos in the areas of morality and religion?

GOD IS RULER

Once God has brought the universe into existence, what is His relationship to its ongoing history? What is His role as Ruler or Lord of all creation?

There are two extremes to be avoided here. One is the idea that God set the universe in motion, then withdrew to let it run according to its own autonomous laws without any further interference from the Creator. This view is usually called deism.

Another unacceptable extreme is the idea that everything

that happens in the ongoing world is actually caused by the Creator — even the so-called "free-will" decisions of human beings. This was John Calvin's view and is usually associated with the theological system called Calvinism. It is alleged that this view alone preserves the sovereignty of God over His creation.

The Biblical view, which is quite different from either of these extremes, will now be summarized.

The Providence of God

The word *providence* is a general term that refers to the subject at hand, namely, the way in which God is related to the ongoing world. This is usually divided into two categories: God's relation to *nature* and His relation to *history*.

First we may note that God rules over all of nature. In a general sense we can say that He is in constant control of everything that happens here. Some passages of Scripture may even suggest that whatever happens in the sphere of nature (e.g., the weather) is caused by God.

Certainly it is God's power that sustains us and provides for the very existence of our own physical lives, along with the existence of everything else. See Acts 17:28; Matthew 5:45; 10:29; Acts 14:17; Colossians 1:17.

But God is also pictured as controlling natural events such as earthquakes and volcanoes (Psa. 104:32), and snowstorms (Psa. 147:15-18). In Job 37:1-13 the prophet Elihu pictures God as controlling weather patterns and cloud movements to accomplish various purposes, including punishment or correction. He may do these things in a supervisory way, through the general providence of His natural laws. Or if He chooses, He may intervene in an act of special providence, altering the course of nature while still working within these

22

established laws.

It is also clearly taught that God rules over all of history, and is in constant control of everything that happens in this sphere. God's involvement here is different, however, since history includes the free-will decisions and affairs of human beings. In order to respect the integrity of human freedom, God does not actually *cause* anyone to make a certain choice. He is very much involved in *influencing* human decisions, however, and in intervening in other ways.

God's control over world history is seen in Psalm 22:28, "For the kingdom is the Lord's, and He rules over the nations." Daniel 5:21 asserts that "the Most High God is ruler over the realm of mankind, and . . . He sets over it whomever He wishes." See Psalms 33:10-17; 75:6,7; 103:19; Ephesians 1:11.

Some are puzzled by passages that seem to indicate that God actually causes people to make certain decisions, e.g., Joseph's brothers' decision to sell him into slavery (Gen. 45:5; 50:20), Pharaoh's decision to keep the Israelites in Egypt (Exod. 4:21; Rom. 9:17,18), and Judas' decision to betray Jesus (Acts 2:23; 4:27,28). Proverbs 21:1 says, "The king's heart is like channels of water in the hand of the Lord; He turns it wherever He wishes."

These passages are not suggesting that God forces people to make specific decisions (even evil ones). They do teach that God is in complete control of the circumstances of every situation. He can manipulate these circumstances in a way that influences certain individuals to make choices that carry out His purposes. Through His foreknowledge of a person's character (e.g., Judas — Acts 2:23) He knows what decisions will be made when certain circumstances are present.

Thus God's involvement in human affairs must be seen in

terms of *control*, not determination or causation. God can *influence* decisions by controlling external circumstances; He can *prevent* their being carried out in the same way. Or He can simply *permit* things to happen according to "natural law" or creaturely decision. This is the Biblical concept of the sovereignty of God.

The Will of God

Can we say, then, that "whatever happens is the will of God"? Yes, but not in the same sense each time. The term "will of God" may mean God's *preceptive* will, which refers to His commandments and laws (Mark 3:35; Matt. 7:21). Obviously many things happen that are contrary to God's will in this sense.

The term may also refer to God's *purposive* will, i.e., the eternal plan and purpose that God determined to carry out from the beginning. Whatever is required to accomplish this purpose, God actually and infallibly causes it to happen. But some things do not affect God's purpose one way or the other and thus are not within His will in this sense. See Ephesians 1:3-1l; 3:8-1l; Hebrews 10:7-9; I Peter 1:18-20.

The term may also refer to God's *permissive* will, or the things He allows and permits to happen. Anything that does not hinder His purposive will — even if it is contrary to His preceptive will (i.e., sinful) — happens within God's permissive will. Everything is within God's control or will, at least in this sense. God may not cause a person to make a certain decision, but he can certainly prevent its being carried out. See James 4:13-15; I Corinthians 16:7; Hebrews 6:3.

The Nature of God

What is the nature of the God who rules the universe in

this fashion? He certainly must be present within His universe (i.e., immanent). God is transcendent; but this merely means that He is different from His creation, not spatially separated or distant from it. See Acts 17:27,28; Psalm 139:7-10.

God must also be completely sovereign, i.e., in absolute control over all creation. This includes His omnipotence (already mentioned) and His omniscience, or His complete and infinite knowledge of all things past, present, and future. It is God's absolute knowledge (including foreknowledge) that enables Him to be in control at all times. See Psalm 147:5; I John 3:20; Isaiah 41:21-23.

The God who rules the universe is also good. See Psalms 36:6; 145:9,15,16; 148; Matthew 5:45. This includes His love: He does not use His omnipotence to torment or to deceive. It also includes His faithfulness: He is able and willing to bless us and to keep His promises and to carry out His purpose of redemption.

CHAPTER THREE

Truth About
God
Our Redeemer

The work of God as Redeemer is the main subject of the Bible; it is also the main theme of this book. Thus we need not go into detail here about the work of redemption, since this will be unfolded later.

We should take note of the fact that salvation is not exclusively a Christian idea. Most religions and religious philosophies have some version of the human predicament and the way to be saved from it. Most of these are quite different from the Christian concept, however. In fact, we can say that the Biblical teaching about *redemption* is entirely unique. It alone promises and provides for a salvation that is wholly by grace.

Most other attempts to construct a system of salvation fall into one of two categories: salvation by knowledge or salvation by works. Down through history many individuals and religious systems have decided that the basic cause of man's problems is ignorance; thus they have devised a way of salvation based on knowledge (enlightenment, education). Examples of this approach are Platonism, Gnosticism, and some forms of mysticism.

In most other systems, whatever the concept of man's predicament, the way out of it is achieved only by the individual's works. If a deity is involved, one must work not to offend him. If he is offended, one must work to appease his wrath. Most primitive religions are of this nature. In religions teaching reincarnation, one achieves salvation by being reincarnated into higher and higher forms of existence until finally he reaches the top and does not have to reenter the cycle at all. Such advancements are made only on the basis of works (goodness, piety, service, self-denial).

The Biblical teaching about redemption shows the error and futility of such concepts as these. Man's problem is too serious to be solved by either education or good works. Salvation must come by a radically different route: the grace of God. We can be saved only by "being justified as a gift by His grace through the redemption which is in Christ Jesus" (Rom. 3:24).

In this chapter we are concerned especially with the nature of God as it is displayed in His work of redemption. Just as the very concept of redemption is unique in Christian teaching, so is the nature of the God who accomplishes it.

THE NEED FOR REDEMPTION

One whole side of God's nature is best seen not in the

accomplishment of redemption but rather as that which makes redemption necessary in the first place. We are referring to the holiness of God, which includes His wrath.

In the Bible the term *holy* basically means "separate, set apart." Its primary reference is to the Creator's separation from or difference from His creation by virtue of His being uncreated. (Thus it is another word for transcendence.) But it can also refer to the righteous God's separation from sin, His absolute purity and uprightness, His moral excellence and perfection. The latter connotation is in view here.

"Holy is the Lord our God," says Psalm 99:9. His holy character is a pattern for our lives: "You shall be holy, for I am holy" (I Pet. 1:16). God is the absolute opposite of all sin; He hates sin with a holy passion. The psalmist says of God, "Thou hast loved righteousness, and hated wickedness" (Psa. 45:7). Also, "Thou dost hate all who do iniquity" (Psa. 5:5). See Isaiah 59:2; Habakkuk 1:13; James 1:13.

When confronted with sin, the holy God by His very nature must respond in *wrath*. It is interesting to note that sinners have never been very fond of emphasizing the wrath of God. Modern liberal religion tends to deny the very idea of divine wrath. As one existentialist theologian put it, "Anger in every shape and form is foreign to God, whose mercy is infinite."

It is obvious that this observer is not talking about the God of the Bible, since the Bible from beginning to end depicts God as a God of wrath. Someone has counted about 580 references to divine wrath in the Old Testament, and the New Testament is no less emphatic on the subject. See Isaiah 30:27-31; Ezekiel 7:8-14; John 3:36; Revelation 6:17; 14:19.

Of course, God's wrath is not a fickle and unpredictable temper, an uncontrollable outburst of rage, or an angry fit. It is simply the natural and inevitable response of the holy God against all that is unholy. It is God's justifiable indignation against the sin that contradicts His very nature.

It is God's righteous wrath that makes redemption necessary. Every other aspect of man's predicament pales in significance beside this one: sinners are under the wrath of God and are doomed to "eternal destruction away from the presence of the Lord" (II Thess. 1:9). "Our God is a consuming fire" (Heb. 12:29).

GOD'S DESIRE TO REDEEM US

In light of the Bible's strong emphasis on God's wrath against sinners, we may marvel that He desires to save us at all. But He does: "The Lord is . . . not wishing for any to perish but for all to come to repentance" (II Pet. 3:9). This divine desire for our redemption exhibits more than anything else the unspeakable *love* of God.

Love in its most basic sense is an attitude of good will, an attitude of caring about another's well-being, a benevolent concern for his welfare. This is without question God's basic attitude toward His creatures. As I John 4:8 says, "God is love."

When good will is directed toward those 'who are suffering and miserable and pitiable, it is called *mercy*. When God in His mercy views us in our state of spiritual crisis and need, He necessarily desires to deliver us from it. Other terms for this attribute are lovingkindness and compassion. See Deuteronomy 5:10; Psalms 57:10; 86:5; 136.

We can understand how God would have this kind of concern for us simply as His creatures. But that He still loves us, even though we are sinners, is truly amazing. See Romans

5:1-11; Ephesians 3:19. When love is thus directed even to the unworthy and undeserving, it is called *grace*. Grace is love for the unlovely, favor for those who have forfeited all right to it. Such is our God. See Ephesians 1:6,7; 2:7-9; Romans 3:24.

GOD'S POWER TO REDEEM US

God may be willing to save us, but is He able? Does God have the power to save us? We have already seen what great power is exhibited in creation from nothing and in the sovereign lordship that God exercises over the universe. Surely a God of such power should be able to deal with sin and with sinners.

Surely. But let us remember what kind of power is shown in creation and in providence — sheer strength, "muscle" power. Certainly the all-powerful God could deal with sin through this kind of power alone, by just destroying all evil and evildoers. In the end all unrepentant sinners will indeed suffer a kind of destruction.

But God is not satisfied to deal with sin by this kind of power alone. His love will not allow it. Because of His love and mercy and grace God chooses — and is able — to overcome sin by a different kind of power: not a destroying and banishing power, but a drawing power, a moral power, "heart" power.

In Romans 1:16 Paul says the gospel (of Christ's death and resurrection) is the power of God for salvation. This is true both in its accomplishment and in its proclamation. The gospel is not just a message; it is a deed, an act. It is an act of love, the deepest and most moving love the world will ever know. The cross is love in action, where God's love in a sense is overpowering His own wrath, not by violating it but by satisfying it through the infinite sufferings of His only begotten Son.

No wonder the gospel proclaimed is power — power to convict, to motivate, to move wills and melt hearts. Jesus declared, "And I, if I be lifted up from the earth [on the cross], will draw all men to Myself" (John 12:32). "The word of the cross . . . is the power of God," says Paul (I Cor. 1:18). When we finally grasp just how far the love of God was willing to go to redeem the unlovely, our own hearts are overpowered (in a sense), and we answer His love with our own (I John 4:19).

If we stand in awe before God's creative and providential power, we must marvel even more at His redemptive power, for there is a sense in which it is the greatest power of all. Aesop told a fable in which the wind and the sun were arguing about which was stronger. They agreed to decide the matter by seeing which of them could remove a traveler's cloak from his back. The wind puffed and howled away, but only caused the traveler to draw his cloak tighter around him. Then the sun commenced to exert another kind of power: its warm and quiet radiance, which soon had the wayfarer wiping his brow and removing his cloak.

Our God has both kinds of power, for which we as sinners should be extremely grateful.

THE FACT OF REDEMPTION

The very fact that God has saved us shows us something about His nature. When God accomplished our redemption through Jesus Christ, He was carrying out a plan that He had laid before the foundation of the world (I Pet. 1:18-20); He was keeping a promise first made in the time of Adam and Eve (Gen. 3:15).

That God carried out His plan and kept His promise shows His *faithfulness*. When God makes a promise, He keeps it. We can count on it. See Psalm 89:1; Lamentations 3:22,23; Isaiah 25:1; II Timothy 2:13; Hebrews 10:23. He is firm and reliable, like a rock (Deut. 32:4; Psa. 62:6,7).

The fact of redemption also shows us that God is unchanging, i.e., He is *immutable*. This aspect of the divine nature has suffered all kinds of extreme interpretations. Early Christian theologians, being unduly influenced by Greek philosophy, made God as static and immobile as a granite statue. He was not even allowed to experience emotions, such as sorrow and joy.

There are those on the other hand, such as modern process philosophers and theologians, who picture God as constantly changing and evolving, along with everything else. This view has tremendous appeal in an age when the theory of evolution dominates every field of learning. But like the other, it must be rejected as an unbiblical extreme.

The Bible does teach that God is unchanging: "For I, the Lord, do not change" (Mal. 3:6). See Micah 7:18-20; James 1:17; Hebrews 13:7-9. The basic point of this, however, is again the faithfulness of God: He does not change His mind or His purposes; He is true and faithful. He is not fickle; He is perfectly consistent at all times. This does mean that His nature is constant and immutable, but it does not rule out genuine interaction with His creatures and genuine emotions such as grief and joy.

J.B. Phillips has written an excellent book called *Your God*

Is Too Small, in which he chides us for our inadequate ideas of God. But in a very real sense, all our concepts of God are too small. No matter how great we picture Him to be, we know that in reality He is always greater.

Hallelujah! What a Savior!

CHAPTER FOUR

Truth About
Man

"What is Man . . . ?" asks Psalm 8:4. The popular answer today would be, "Anything he wants to be!" After all, everyone is free to "do his own thing."

This is merely one expression of modern relativism, as underscored by evolutionary theory. Modern man has concluded that there is no such thing as "human nature," that there is no ideal pattern for humanness, no model after which man was made and for which he must strive. Thus science is free to reconstruct man as it pleases (or dares), and any individual is free to live any life-style he chooses.

A current trend in the religious world comes dangerously close to this way of thinking. it is called "relational theology." It asserts that we need not be concerned about the essential nature of anything, not even of God or man; all that matters is relationships. A recent speaker endorsed this notion when he said, "The Bible defines God and man not in the abstract terms of 'nature' but in terms of their relationship to each other."

We must strongly disagree with this approach. It seems to reflect more of the spirit of the age than the teaching of Scripture. It beguiles us with that slippery piece of logical trickery, the false choice. We do not have to choose between essence and relationships; the Bible speaks of both.

There is abundant information in Scripture about the essence or nature of man, what he is in his essential being. This chapter will attempt to summarize this teaching.

WHAT IS MAN "MADE OF"?

A familiar nursery rhyme asks, "What are little girls/boys made of?" Though the answers given are not quite orthodox, the question is a proper one. What *are* human beings "made of"? We are not referring to the various chemical elements of the body or to the various parts like bones and muscles and how they are put together. Rather, we are thinking in terms of the broader components of *matter* and *spirit*.

The Options

What are the options? Since we are working with only two components, there are only three choices: (1) man is spirit only; (2) man is matter only; (3) man is both matter and spirit. There are defenders for all three views.

The view that man is spirit only is much more prevalent than most Westerners realize. For example, Mary Baker Eddy (the founder of the Christian Science cult) says bluntly, "Man is not material; he is spiritual." She indicates that matter itself, including the human body, does not really exist. This view is much more common in Eastern religions such as Hinduism, which views all matter as *maya* (illusion). Only man's spirit is his true nature, and it will one day be rejoined to the great universal spirit from which it was derived. We should be aware, too, that the New Age Movement generally operates with a Hindu view of man and things.

Many Christians come too close to this false idea when they discount the importance of the body and speak of man's spirit as "the real man, the part that counts." It is indeed *a* part that counts, but not the *only* part that counts.

The view that man is matter or body only is much more common in today's world. We are not surprised that secular materialists defend this idea, since they deny *any* kind of spiritual existence, whether it be divine, angelic, or human. But this view is widespread in the religious world as well. That man has no spiritual essence called soul or spirit is a principal teaching of several major cults. Some contemporary liberal Christians teach the same thing, claiming to be following "authentic Hebrew thought" rather than "perverted Greek philosophy." Actually, they have chosen secular materialism over Biblical teaching.

An alarming number of otherwise conservative preachers and teachers give the impression that they are leaning to this "body only" view. Their desire is to correct certain extremes in the "spirit-only" direction. But the cure is as bad as the disease, and Biblical truth is lost in false choices and selective exegesis.

The traditional view that man is both body and spirit is the only view consistent with Biblical teaching. This will now be presented.

Body and Spirit

The Bible uses a variety of terms to refer to man's physical nature, including *sheath*, *outer man*, *body*, and *flesh*. (It is important to note that the word *flesh*, especially in Paul's writings, often has another connotation. In such passages as Romans 8:1-13 and Galatians 5:16-21 it refers not to the body as such, but to the old sinful self or sinful way of life. As such it is contrasted with the Holy Spirit, who is the source of our new life and life-style.)

There are also several terms for man's spiritual nature, including *heart, inner man, spirit*, and *soul*. (Some think there is a difference between soul and spirit, in view of such passages as I Thessalonians 5:23 and Hebrews 4:12. If there is a difference, it certainly receives little attention in Scripture, and we should not try to draw any far-reaching theological conclusions from it. A better understanding of these passages and of Scripture as a whole is that the terms *soul* and *spirit* are synonyms when they are used to describe man's spiritual nature.)

That human nature is a combination of material and spiritual elements is the overwhelming impression we get when we read both the Old and New Testaments. Daniel 7:15 says literally, "My spirit was distressed in the midst of its sheath." Ecclesiastes 12:7 says, "The dust will return to the earth as it was, and the spirit will return to God who gave it." The Old Testament also describes man as heart and flesh (Ezek. 44:7,9; Eccl. 11:10; Psalm 16:9), and soul and flesh (Psa. 63:1). See also Psalm 31:9; Ezekiel 21:7; Isaiah 10:18.

The New Testament is even clearer. Man is described as spirit and flesh (Matt. 26:41; II Cor. 7:1), as spirit and body (Rom. 8:10; I Cor. 7:34; James 2:26), and as soul and body

(Matt. 10:28). Paul contrasts the outward man and the inward man (II Cor. 4:16; see I Pet. 3:3,4). Jesus makes it very clear in Matthew 10:28 that soul and body are distinct and separable entities: "And do not fear those who kill the body, but are unable to kill the soul; but rather fear Him who is able to destroy both soul and body in hell." The *souls* of those whose bodies have died continue to exist (Revelation 6:9), though "unclothed" until the resurrection (II Cor. 5:4) when they are to receive new, spiritual bodies.

Some confusion arises from the fact that certain key Hebrew and Greek words have more than one meaning. For instance, the words translated *spirit* can also mean "breath" or "wind." But this does not mean that they always mean either breath or wind. (Should we begin speaking of the "Holy Breath"?) Also, the words translated *soul* can have other meanings, especially "life" (John 10:11; Matt. 16:25) and "person" or "self" (Acts 2:41; Rom. 13:1). But again, these are not their only meanings. Only the context can tell us whether the word for *soul* actually means "life" or "person" or "spiritual nature." In some places it can only mean "spiritual nature" (Matt. 10:28; Rev. 6:9), but in the passages cited above it is properly translated "life" or "person."

The conclusion is that man is a twofold creature, designed by God to be both material and spiritual. Each is part of the essential nature of man; if either is missing man is not whole.

Implications

Man's dual nature has a number of very important implications. First, we would note that man is *body*. He was created with a body that was never intended to die. Man's physical nature is good, not evil, alien, or accidental — though this latter view is a very influential pagan notion. But contrary to such pagan ideas, the body is not a tomb or a prison from which the "real self" (the spirit) longs to escape. Bodily existence is part of our very essence; God intends for us to have bodies forever, and He will provide them for us.

Second, Man is *spirit*. There is definitely a nonmaterial aspect to our being, which makes us distinct from every other creature in the material universe. Man is qualitatively different from animals. Being spirit, we are like God, who is Spirit. We must be very cautious here. Our spirits are *like* God, but not *exactly* like Him. God alone is uncreated Spirit; men (and angels) are *created* spirits. Contrary to much pagan thought, man's soul or spirit is not a little part of God; it is not divine. This means that the soul is not inherently eternal or immortal. It was created, and it could be annihilated if God chose to annihilate it. (But He does not so choose.) We need not, however, choose between an "immortal soul" and no soul. This is a false choice that "body-only" advocates often try to force upon us.

A final implication is that man is a *unity* of body and spirit. Both are necessary for human wholeness. Reflecting on this unity yields several conclusions:

1. Body and spirit are not "natural enemies." They do not need a third entity to hold them together (i.e., a "soul" as distinct from spirit).

2. Man is just as genuinely body as he is spirit. Both are the "real man."

3. Sin affects the whole man, body and spirit.

4. Death is abnormal (for one thing) because it divides the whole man, separating soul from body. The "intermediate state" (when the soul is in Paradise "unclothed") is not yet a perfect state.

5. Salvation involves the whole man, body and spirit.

Salvation is not just an escape from the body. We do not just save people's "souls." Their bodies are redeemed too (Rom. 8:23).

6. Man as a unity of body and spirit is uniquely equipped to relate both to God and to the world. Because we are material, the universe is our natural environment. But because we are also spirit, we have dominion over it (Gen. 1:26-28). On the other hand, because we are spirit, we can naturally worship and fellowship with God. But because we are flesh, such worship sometimes is properly accomplished via material means (e.g., bread and juice, or musical instruments).

IN THE IMAGE OF GOD

A unique aspect of man's nature is the fact that he is created "in the image of God" (Gen. 1:26,27). What does this mean? Basically it means that we are persons; we have personhood.

Personhood is the essence of spiritual existence. Spiritual beings are personal beings. This is what makes us like God. God is Spirit; we are spirit. God is personal; we are personal.

As persons we have the capacity for interpersonal relationships not only with one another but with God Himself. This is God's supreme design for man; this is why God made us in His image. Only when we are in a right personal relationship with God are we fulfilling our purpose as human beings.

We may note several implications. First, every human being possesses an inherent dignity, meaning, and worth. This is true of the lowest and meanest person on earth, as well as the noblest. It is the ground for self-respect.

Second, we must have a unique respect for human life.

Schweitzer's philosophy of reverence for all forms of life denies the qualitative distinction between human life and all other life. Only human life is protected by God's law (Exod. 20:13). The very fact that man is in God's image is what makes murder so foul and capital punishment so proper (Gen. 9:6).

Finally, we must have a sincere desire to evangelize the lost. When a human being dies unsaved it means that another person made in God's image will spend eternity in hell. Could there be a greater tragedy?

CHAPTER FIVE

Truth About
Sin

Read Genesis 1:31. "And God saw all that he had made, and behold, it was very good." Now read any history book. Read about the horrors of the Babylonian and Roman sieges of Jerusalem. Read about the Nazi and Cambodian holocausts. This is "very good"?

Pick up the newspaper. Read about current wars and mass murders and torture-killings. Read about alcoholics and dope addicts and prostitutes. Read about terrorism, overcrowded prisons, and abortions by the million. This is "very good"?

Clearly something has gone wrong. Surely the world we see is not the world that God declared to be "very good." Surely the human race that has filled history books with violence and gore and filth is not the same as the perfect pair that graced Eden. What has happened?

The answer is that an alien has invaded our universe and corrupted it to the core. That alien is sin. It entered through the hearts of Adam and Eve as recorded in Genesis 3, and nothing has been the same since.

It is extremely important that we have a proper understanding of the doctrine of sin. We especially need to know what effect sin has had upon us. We need to know the nature of the predicament into which sin has brought us. This will be our focus in this chapter.

ADAM'S SIN

The question of how sin has affected us is complicated by an additional question, namely, *whose* sin has affected us? Do we wrestle only with our own sin, or do we also receive some unwanted legacy from our first parents, Adam and Eve?

Here we are dealing with the serious problem of "original sin." Did the original sin of Adam (shorthand for Adam and Eve) have any kind of effect on the human race as a whole? This question has received a multitude of different answers. Let's glance at some of them.

A Variety of Views

At one end of the spectrum, some have said that Adam's sin affected us only indirectly in that it changed our environment. With sin now all around us, we become sinners by imitation.

Others have said that Adam's sin brought the whole race under the curse of physical death, but it did not affect our *spiritual* condition in any way. We are born mortal, but are innocent and pure until we imitate Adam and commit our own sin. (This and the previous view are forms of *Pelagianism*.)

Still others agree that we die physically because of Adam's sin, and that we inherit no guilt from Adam and are thus born innocent. But, they say, we do inherit a weakened and sullied spiritual nature, a tendency to sin. This limited depravity makes it probable that we will sin, but not necessary. (This view is often called *semi-Pelagianism*.)

Traditional Roman Catholicism carries this view a step further by affirming that even guilt and eternal punishment are upon our heads even before we are born, because of Adam's sin.

The most extreme view is one invented by Augustine in the early fifth century A.D. (Thus it is called *Augustinianism*, and sometimes *Calvinism*.) This is the complete classical doctrine of original sin. In addition to physical death, according to this view the entire human race "inherits" or receives from Adam a whole package of spiritual problems. First, every baby is born guilty and condemned to hell. Second, each child is born with a depraved spiritual nature. Third, this depravity is so *total* that the infant has lost his free will: he grows up totally unable to choose to do good. This last item is called "total depravity" or "bondage of the will." Bible-believing Lutherans and Calvinists (Presbyterians and Reformed churches) hold to this view.

Romans 5:12-21

As strange as it may seem, most of these views do claim to be the true Biblical teaching. Most of them even appeal to the same passage of Scripture (among others) as the primary source of their doctrine: Rom. 5:12-21. Here Paul says that "through one man sin entered into the world, and death through sin" (verse 12). Also, "through one transgression there resulted condemnation to all men" (verse 18), and "through the one man's disobedience the many were made sinners" (verse 19).

These statements are taken by some to mean physical death only, and by others to include also a limited depravity. Augustinians find the whole package included here: physical death, spiritual death (total depravity, to them), and eternal death (condemnation to hell).

What is Paul actually teaching in this difficult passage? At the very least he seems to say we all die physically because of Adam's sin. But is he saying more? Do the terms "condemnation" and "sinners" in verses 18 and 19 refer to inherited (or imputed) guilt and depravity?

We answer, "Perhaps; perhaps not." But wait! How can we be so casual and indecisive about such a critical question? Because, in the final analysis, it *really doesn't matter*! That is to say, it really doesn't matter what the human race got from Adam, because whatever it was is removed or canceled out by the redemptive work of Jesus Christ! This is the whole point of the passage, especially verses 15-19. It is summed up concisely by A.I. Hobbs: "What, without our will or consent, we lost in the first Adam, we have regained or shall regain in the second Adam, without our will or consent."

Do we die because of Adam's sin? No matter: "in Christ all shall be made alive" (I Cor. 15:22). Do guilt and even total depravity fall potentially upon all people because of Adam's sin? No matter: they are canceled out for the whole human race by Christ's "one act of righteousness" (Rom. 5:18), even before they take effect, even for those ones who lived before the cross.

Thus in the final analysis, no one suffers any permanent

consequences of Adam's sin. Christ's redemptive work matches Adam's sin point for point, canceling its sting. Whatever guilt and depravity we possess now are ours because of our own personal sin, not Adam's. If our physical death is not nullified by redemptive resurrection, it is because we have forfeited it anew through our own personal sin. But, praise God, Christ's saving grace can take care of all this, too: this is the "much more" Paul is emphasizing in the passage (vv. 15,17).

PERSONAL SIN

What we should be concerned with, then, are not the consequences of Adam's sin, but the consequences of our own sin. How has our own personal sin affected us spiritually? It has caused us two basic problems.

Our Sin Makes Us Guilty

The first result of personal sin against God is that it makes us guilty. By definition sin is lawlessness or transgression of the law (I John 3:4). Violation of the law's precepts makes us liable to the law's penalty. It is the most serious penalty imaginable (eternal hell) because sin is the most serious offense possible. To break God's law is to rebel against Him personally; it is an insult against His wisdom and authority.

Thus our first problem is a legal one. Sin brings us into a wrong relationship to God's law; we are "in trouble with the law." God's eternal justice requires the penalty to be imposed in order to uphold the law's integrity. The Judge says, "Guilty!" and the sentence is pronounced: judgment, wrath, punishment, condemnation, damnation, death.

Let us remember that we do not inherit this guilt from Adam. Babies are not born guilty. We become guilty and liable to punishment only when we have become old enough to understand what it means to sin against God. Then we become accountable for our own sin and no one else's. Ezekiel 18:4 expresses this principle of individual responsibility: "The soul [person] who sins will die." Each person is recompensed according to his own works (not someone else's). See Psalm 62:12; Romans 14:12; II Corinthians 5:10.

Our Sin Makes Us Sick

As if it weren't bad enough to become guilty from our sin, we also bring upon ourselves another problem: spiritual sickness, corruption, weakness, depravity, sinfulness. The sinner's soul (heart, spirit) becomes diseased with sin. Thus sin corrupts not just our relationships with God and His law; it corrupts our very natures. "Sin is not only what we do, but also what we are" (Buswell). *Sins* are sinful; *sinners* are sinful.

Jesus makes this clear when He says that both the tree and the fruit (i.e., our natures and our deeds) are corrupt (Matt. 7:17; 12:33-35). He speaks of evil *men,* not just evil deeds (Matt. 5:39,45; 12:34,35). This corruption is in the heart (inner man, spirit): "The heart is more deceitful than all else and is desperately sick" (Jeremiah 17:9). Bodily sickness is often used as an analogy of our soul's condition. See Isaiah 1:5,6; Romans 3:10-18.

This sickness is serious enough to be called *death,* a deadness of the soul. See Ephesians 2:1,5; I Timothy 5:6; Jude 12. (Note that Ephesians says we are dead in *our own* sins, not Adam's.)

What does this mean? It means that the more we sin, the harder it is not to sin. Our souls are infested with the open sores of evil thoughts, lust, jealousy, covetousness, and hatred; and we can't seem to make them go away. Our weakened wills are unable to resist temptation. Our hearts are hardened in rebellion against God, and blinded to His truth. McGarvey calls it "that helpless weakness of sin" that makes us powerless to please God. We are in the grip of the *power* of sin.

Some use the word *depravity* to describe this sinful condition. The only problem is that most people associate this term with the Augustinian concept of total depravity. We have already rejected the notion that everyone is *born* totally depraved as the result of Adam's sin. But apart from that question, many still insist that the Bible teaches that sinners *are* totally depraved. We believe this to be a false view, one whose presence in Christian thinking has had the direst results. Thus we will give a brief explanation and refutation of it.

For those who hold this view, total depravity does not mean that a sinner is as depraved as he possibly can be. It means that the total man is depraved: heart, mind, emotions, will, every part. The key element is the bondage of the will, which results in a *total inability* to do anything good in God's sight. Especially, say those who hold this view, the sinner cannot respond to the gospel and turn to God in faith and repentance. His depravity makes this impossible. Thus a sinner will never believe and be saved unless God regenerates him (changes his heart) first, apart from the sinner's choice and decision and faith.

The Biblical passages that are supposed to teach this idea in reality do not. For instance, passages such as Jeremiah 17:9 and Ephesians 2:1, which do teach that sinners are sick and depraved, are used to prove this view. But depravity as such is not the same as *total* depravity.

Other passages (e.g., Rom. 8:7,8; Jer. 13:23) do teach that a sinner is not able to do good works. But this refers to his efforts to live a good life per se, and does not include turning to God in faith. Without faith it is impossible to please God (Heb. 11:6). Thus as long as one refuses to believe in Christ, as long as his mind is set on sinful things, nothing he does can be good before God. But he *can* turn to God, trusting His promises and receiving new power for obedience.

But doesn't the Bible say that no one can turn to God unless God draws him? (John 6:44,65). Yes, but this drawing is not by some secret, selective process; it is accomplished by the power of the gospel (Rom. 10:17; James 1:18; John 12:32). One of the very purposes of the written Word is to lead to faith (John 20:31). God does draw sinners, but the drawing is universal and resistible.

But isn't faith a *gift*? and repentance too? See Acts 5:31; 11:18; 13:48; Philippians 1:29; Ephesians 2:8,9, and elsewhere. In one sense, faith is a gift, in that God gives us the *opportunity* to believe and repent. But a gift given is not necessarily a gift received. Some accept the gift; some reject it. It is not given selectively and irresistibly. But in the strict sense, neither faith nor the ability to believe is a special gift. (Ephesians 2:8,9 should be carefully exegeted. The "gift of God" mentioned here is not faith. Simple Greek grammar rules out this idea.)

A key passage that refutes the total depravity doctrine is Colossians 2:12, which says that in baptism we were "raised up" (regenerated, born again, made alive) *through faith*. This shows that faith is already present before the Holy Spirit regenerates us. Faith must precede regeneration. This is just the opposite of the total depravity idea, which requires regeneration to precede faith.

In rejecting total depravity let us not lose sight of the fact that our own sin *has* made us sick (yes, depraved) in a serious though limited way, just as it has made us guilty. This is our "double trouble," the two problems that redemption must solve.

CHAPTER SIX

Truth About
Death

Pieces of plastic or chunks of granite are not alive, but we wouldn't call them "dead" either. That they lack life is irrelevant, since they never were alive and never were intended to be.

If something is dead, this implies that in its normal state it is intended to be alive. Death is the absence of life, the withdrawal of the principle of life, separation from the source of life.

It is clear that man is intended to be alive. The living God made man as a "living being" (Gen. 2:7) with the intention that he should live forever in fellowship with his Maker. But when sin entered so did death (Gen. 2:17; Rom. 5:12). Man the living creature became man the dying creature.

Truly, "the wages of sin is death" (Rom. 6:23). It might be

said, though, that these wages are paid in different kinds of currency. That is to say, there are different kinds of death, three in all.

First, there is *physical* death. Man is intended to be a unity of spirit and body. As long as the two are united, the body is alive. Man's spirit is the source for his bodily life. James 2:26 says that "the body without the spirit is dead." Physical death occurs when the spirit is separated from the body. (See John 19:30.)

Second, there is *spiritual* death. This is equivalent to the state of spiritual depravity discussed in the preceding chapter, a state referred to as "death" (Eph. 2:1,5; Col. 2:13). The sinner's soul is truly dead, because it has become separated from its source of life, which is God himself (Eph. 4:18). The sinner is in a state of separation from God (Isa. 59:2); his spiritual life is gone. (When he returns to God and is converted, he becomes alive again. Ephesians 2:5.)

Finally, there is *eternal* death. On the Day of Judgment the condemned sinner will be cast, body and soul (Matt. 10:28), into the eternal lake of fire, which is called the "second death" (Rev. 20:14,15; 21:8). The essence of this death is not annihilation or nonexistence, but eternal, irreversible separation from God. See Matthew 7:23; 22:13; 25:41; II Thessalonians 1:7-10.

The remainder of this chapter will focus upon the Bible's teaching about only one of these: physical death. We will see how physical death is described as a penalty for sin, an enemy to be feared, and an enemy that has been defeated by Jesus Christ.

DEATH IS A PENALTY

"Why do people die?" Modern man's answer to this question is, "Why not? Everything else dies."

This answer assumes that man is a part of the natural order in the same way that everything else is. This is part of the Trojan-horse legacy of evolutionary theory: human life evolved by the same process as all other life; human death thus is as natural as insect death or elephant death.

Some church leaders have readily absorbed this view of death. One commonly hears, even from Bible-believing Christians, the idea that death is natural, and that it is not the result of sin. As one writer puts it, "Mortal death is not related to sin but is a part of the created order from the beginning."

How wrong this is! The Bible clearly teaches that human physical death is definitely the result of and even the penalty for human sin. In the beginning Adam and Eve were warned: if you disobey, "you shall surely die" (Gen. 2:17).) In Romans 1:32 Paul says that those who practice sin are "worthy of death." Paul also declares that death is the wages of sin, and that "the body is dead because of sin" (Rom. 6:23; 8:10). James 1:15 lists the genealogy of death thus: "When lust has conceived, it gives birth to sin; and when sin is accomplished, it brings forth death."

Romans 5:12 explains that death entered into the world and spread to all men through one man, Adam. That is, individuals do not die as the penalty for some personal sin that they have committed. It is a curse upon the whole race, so that even infants and saints die. (Whether an individual is redemptively raised from death does depend upon whether he has sinned personally and then upon whether he has been saved by Christ from his personal sins.)

In any case it is quite plain that human death is not natural and normal. Man was not created with the intention or assumption that he would just naturally die, like everything else. Only when sin entered did the curse of death fall upon mankind. It is the penalty for sin.

A common response is that these passages are talking about spiritual and/or eternal death, but not physical death. We grant that the other aspects of death are probably in view, but it is quite impossible to say that these passages do not intend to include physical death also. For instance, in Genesis 2:17 the penalty for disobedience is death; and when this penalty is imposed (Gen. 3:19), the only kind of death mentioned is physical death. We must read Romans 5:12 in light of the total context (e.g., Rom. 6:9), which shows that physical death is in view. Romans 8:10 specifically relates sin to the death of the body.

Some considerations related to salvation also make the same point. For instance, the fact that the resurrection of the body is an act of redemption (Rom. 8:23) shows that the death of the body is the result of sin. Also, if physical death is natural, in what sense can Christ's death on the cross be a curse? See Galatians 3:13; Hebrews 2:14,15.

People die because of sin. Let us not succumb to the devil's lie that these two things are unrelated (see Gen. 3:4).

DEATH IS AN ENEMY

When a person dies he is not just "doing what comes naturally." Rather, he has been overtaken and overwhelmed by an alien attacker that has pursued him since his conception. He has fallen (at least temporarily) to his relentless enemy, death.

It is quite proper to think of death as an *enemy* — an enemy to dread, to fight, and to conquer. Hebrews 2:14,15 speaks of Satan as having the "power of death" and of death itself as a captor that holds people in bondage through fear. In Matthew 16:18 Jesus pictures the church as a refuge or fortress that protects us from the onslaught of death. (Here the "gates of *Hades*" — the place of death — symbolize death's power to overwhelm its victims.) First Corinthians 15:25,26 describes death as "the last enemy" to be defeated by Christ (in the final resurrection).

Thus we should never "make friends" with death; we should never be complacent or nonchalant about it. We cannot agree with the Christian editor who writes about "the illusion of death as terrible." It has never had the terror that men associate with it, he says. Rather, it is "an appointment of the gracious God." The reference to the "valley of the shadow of death" (Psa. 23:4) means just that: death is only a shadow, an illusion, an "appearance without substance," he says.

This kind of thinking obscures the fact that sinners definitely should fear death, because it is part of the penalty for sin, and because it is the prelude to the final judgment (Heb. 9:27). After all, "it is a terrifying thing to fall into the hands of the living God" (Heb. 10:31).

Many current movements are working overtime, under Satanic inspiration, to convince the world that death is natural and harmless, even that it is beautiful and friendly. Evolutionary theory has been most successful in accomplishing this end. Occultism also preaches this message, especially in its form of spiritism. The main message of spiritism is "there is no death": it's nothing; it's just a door you pass through.

A most deceitful spin-off from modern spiritism is the popular "life-after-life" movement, led by Raymond Moody and Elisabeth Kübler-Ross (whose spiritist connections are no secret). The main message of this controversial cult seems to be, "Death is a friend — don't fear it." The majority of those who have the life-after-life experience return convinced that death is beautiful and blessed for all, regardless of their religious beliefs.

Whatever the explanation of these experiences, the conclusions being drawn from them are often Satanic and anti-Biblical. They deny the gospel of Christ. We must be on guard against this and every effort of Satan to get us to make friends with that "last enemy," death.

DEATH IS A DEFEATED ENEMY

Someone will now say, "But I thought Christians were not supposed to fear death." This is quite true. We have been delivered from the fear of death (Heb. 2:14,15), but not by the lie that death is a friend. Our deliverance has come through the gospel message, which says, "Our enemy death has been defeated!" Death is still an enemy, but because of Jesus Christ it is a *defeated* enemy. In His cross and resurrection Jesus conquered death (Rev. 1:17,18). If we belong to Christ, we share this victory. This is why we no longer fear death.

We do a terrible disservice to unbelievers when we endorse in any way the idea that death is normal, natural, and friendly. (We must be very careful what we say at deathbeds and funerals.) Anyone outside of Christ's saving grace should stand in terror before death and the judgment that follows it. Of course we want them to be free from this terror, but we must make it clear that the only true escape from it is by accepting the Christian gospel. See Hebrews 2:14,15 again.

The whole story of redemption is God's solution to the problem of death — spiritual, eternal, and physical. Christ's saving work delivers us from the penalty, power, and fear of death. This is what Christianity is all about! This is the glory of the gospel! Let us not rob the gospel of its glory by mistaking a defeated enemy for an old friend.

CHAPTER SEVEN

Truth About
Grace

"Why do you think you should go to Heaven?"

At some point in his life every person surely gives some thought to the certainty or at least the possibility of a Judgment Day. Then the question arises: "Will I pass? Will I actually be allowed into Heaven?"

Suppose the Judge were to question you in just that way: "Why should you be allowed into Heaven?" What would you say? What do you think God would want you to say? What kind of speech would God have to hear to reply, "OK. That's good enough. Go on in"?

This raises the question of the very nature of salvation. By what process does a person qualify for Heaven? If Heaven can be thought of as a destination, what route must one take to get there? If Heaven can be compared to a prize given to the winner of a game, how does one win? What are the ground rules that determine the outcome of the game?

This is the context in which grace can best be understood. Given man's predicament as described in the last two chapters, is it possible to devise a plan to save him from it? Yes, it is possible, but only if we approach the problem in terms of grace. Grace describes the basic character of salvation, the nature of the whole approach to the project of getting sinners into Heaven.

Thus if we are going to have the right speech ready for that critical Judgment-Day question, we must formulate it from within the system of grace. We must begin to adjust our thought-patterns to think in terms of grace. How important it is, then, that we understand what grace is all about!

GRACE: THE SPIRIT OF GIVING

First we would note that grace is the *spirit of giving*. In its most general connotation the Greek word for grace refers to that which brings joy and gladness to the heart. The connection with gifts and giving is then most natural. One theological dictionary says that the starting point for the meaning of grace is "making glad by gifts." It is a "gift that makes glad."

This meaning is especially significant when we see that grace is the basis for salvation. It helps us to see the nature of the process by which God delivers us from sin's consequences. It shows the fundamental distinction between being lost and being saved.

Romans 6:23 says, "For the wages of sin is death, but the free gift of God is eternal life." Here we see the opposite destinations of the lost (death) and the saved (life). But we also see a sharp contrast between the two ways or methods of determining these destinies. Death is described as the *wages* of sin; i.e., the sinner gets what his works and manner of life deserve. He gets what he has earned, what is owed to him. But eternal life is called God's *free gift*. It is not something earned; we have no rightful claim to it. It is something to be had only in the form of a gift. This is the way grace operates. See Ephesians 2:8.

Here is the starting point for understanding grace. It has to do with giving, in contrast with earning or deserving. "According to grace" is the opposite of "according to debt" (Rom. 4:4).

GRACE: AN ATTITUDE OF GOD

Grace as the spirit of giving cannot be just an abstract principle or an impersonal object kept in a box in a closet. It is something that exists first of all as a disposition in the giver's heart. It is an attitude or frame of mind; it is the desire and willingness to give.

This is where "the grace of God that brings salvation" (Titus 2:11, NIV) begins: in the very heart of God. Grace is a divine disposition, an *attitude of God.*

We have already seen that holiness is a divine disposition, too. This means that God does indeed treat us as we deserve. We are sinners, and sin deserves condemnation and wrath. Thus God, being a just God, condemns us and pours out His wrath upon us. "For He pays a man according to his work . . . the Almighty will not pervert justice" (Job 34:11,12). See Romans 12:19; Ezekiel 7:8,9; Hebrews 12:29.

But there is another side to God's nature. The same God

who is a "consuming fire" is also loving, merciful, and gracious. In fact, God's disposition of love prevails (in a sense) over His wrath, in that His grace provides a way for sinners to escape from wrath. His wrath is real, but it is not His "final" word. "Has God forgotten to be gracious?" (Psa. 77:9) No! "The Lord is compassionate and gracious, slow to anger and abounding in lovingkindness" (Psa. 103:8). "Who is a God like Thee, who pardons iniquity and passes over the rebellious act . . . ? He does not retain His anger forever, because He delights in unchanging love" (Micah 7:18).

This means that God will rightfully pay us what we deserve (the wages of sin) if we are content to let His holiness or justice prevail. But it also means that He can — and would rather — treat us contrary to what we deserve. In other words, He desires to be gracious toward us, if we will only allow Him. (God gives grace only to those who are willing to receive it. See Matt. 23:37.)

This is the essence of grace. In a sense it is the opposite of justice. God loves us even though we do not deserve His love; He has provided a salvation that we cannot earn and of which we cannot be worthy. Contrary to what we *ought* to receive, God offers us the *gift* of eternal life.

GRACE: A WAY OF SALVATION

Corresponding to the two basic attitudes of God (holiness and love), there are two ways of relating to God. Picture it this way. Think of God (for purposes of illustration only) as sitting in Heaven. In His throne room there are two windows through which He can see all mankind. One window is His holiness; all those whom He views through this window will be paid what they have earned. The other window is His gracious love; all those whom He sees here will receive, as a gift, the opposite of what they deserve.

Here we are actually talking about two (possible) ways of getting into Heaven. One is the way of law, the other is the way of grace. (See John 1:17; Gal. 5:4; Rom. 6:14.) Under the system of law we relate to God in terms of His holiness; under the system of grace we relate to Him in terms of His love.

How we answer the question, "Why should you be admitted to Heaven?" depends on whether we are trying to get in by law or by grace. The difference is all-important, and we want to make it clear.

The Way of Law

Law as a way of salvation is not difficult to understand. Its ground rules are quite simple: "Keep the commandments; escape the penalty. Break the commandments; suffer the penalty."

The word *commandments* refers to the code of laws or commands that applies in the age into which a person is born. If a person keeps the commands that apply to him, he will escape God's wrath and be saved. If he breaks the commands, he will suffer the penalty. This is how the law system operates.

We have no choice about beginning our lives under law. This is the natural state of things. Every person is born under law as a way of relating to God, as well as under a particular law code (such as the Mosaic law, or New Testament rules). Everyone must respond to the commands that apply to him, either by keeping them or by breaking them.

Now, it is theoretically possible to be saved under law. The ground rules specify, "Keep the commandments; escape the penalty." Thus under law one can be saved *if* he keeps the commandments. But he must keep *all* of them — perfectly. Only perfect obedience deserves Heaven. One sin and all is lost. See James 2:10; Galatians 3:10.

Will anyone actually get into Heaven by way of law (i.e., law-keeping)? The answer is no, because "all have sinned" (Romans 3:23). Thus not a single person will be saved according to the rules of law. As long as we continue to relate to God in terms of law, we can only expect to receive the penalty we deserve.

The Way of Grace

The essence of the gospel is that there is another way to relate to God, another way to get into Heaven: the way of grace. It is a totally different system. It operates by an entirely different set of ground rules. Salvation is provided according to these terms: "Keep the commandments, but suffer the penalty. Break the commandments, but escape the penalty."

"But wait a minute," someone objects. "Isn't there something wrong here? Why should one who keeps the commandments suffer the penalty, and the one who breaks them escape? That doesn't seem fair!"

This is absolutely correct. It is *not* fair. It is not supposed to be. If it were fair, it would not be grace! Law is fair. Grace is something very different from "fair."

"OK," comes the reply, "but there is one more thing. The second statement, 'Break the commandments, but escape the penalty,' is great. That's our only hope. But what about that first rule: 'Keep the commandments, but suffer the penalty'? Surely this is going too far. How can that be grace?"

Admittedly, this seems very odd and even objectionable.

But remember, grace is different from our ordinary way of thinking. It does not fit within the framework of law and justice and fairness. This is especially true of the first statement.

But this is the very element of grace that makes it grace! Without this provision, the other one would be impossible. After all, to whom does this provision apply? Who has kept the commandments perfectly, anyway? Only one person: Jesus Christ. But even though He kept the commandments, He suffered the penalty. Why? For grace! Only the demands of grace could nail our spotless Lord to the cross. For in His sinless death He suffered the full penalty of law *in our place*, and thus made it possible for us as actual lawbreakers to escape the penalty.

The system of grace is summed up perfectly in II Corinthians 5:21, "He made Him who knew no sin to be sin on our behalf, that we might become the righteousness of God in Him." Christ took our sins, and we receive His righteousness. God treated Jesus like a sinner, so that we can be treated like sinless ones. In this way God's holiness is satisfied (the penalty is paid), but so is His love !

Thus under grace, because of Jesus, we can escape the penalty, even though we have sinned. We are not treated as we deserve. We relate to God according to grace, not law. We claim His love, and escape His wrath.

(Remember: the law-grace distinction is not the same as the distinction between the Old and New Testaments. What has been said here applies in any age. No sinner can be saved by lawkeeping, whether it be the Mosaic Law or New Testament commandments).

Whether a person relates to God according to law or according to grace is his own choice. He can choose to remain under law and be treated as he deserves. In this case, when God asks, "Why should I let you into Heaven?" he will answer like the Pharisee (was he rehearsing for the Judgment Day?): "Because I have obeyed all your commandments" (Luke 18:11,12). This of course is not true, but what else can one say when he bases his hope on law-keeping? Like the Pharisee, he will be lost (v. 14).

Or a person can realize that grace is his only hope, and get ready to answer with the publican, "God, be merciful to me, the sinner!" (v. 13). This is what God wants to hear us say, because this is the only way He can save us.

CHAPTER EIGHT

Truth About
Jesus Christ

"Christianity is Christ," someone has said. Indeed this is true. The entire Biblical message of salvation revolves around and rests upon Jesus Christ. He alone makes the gospel of grace possible. He alone has delivered us from sin's penalty. He alone has conquered death. He alone makes anything else in this book worth writing or reading.

The Biblical teaching about Jesus is the pinnacle of Christian doctrine, the most sublime and glorious doctrine in Scripture. No truth taught in the Bible should thrill the sinner's heart and give him more joy than its truth about Jesus Christ.

Realizing the limitations imposed by space, we shall now try to answer in brief form the two basic questions about Jesus: Who is He? and What did He do? (These subjects are called the *person* and the *work* of Christ.) These two questions are answered concisely, in reverse order, in Peter's famous confession at Caesarea Philippi: "Thou art the Christ, the Son of the living God" (Matt. 16:16).

JESUS IS THE CHRIST

All Christians, along with Peter, joyfully confess that Jesus is the Christ. What does this mean? The word *Christ* is the same as the word *Messiah*; it means "the anointed one." In the context of the Old Testament, anointing is the equivalent of being ordained to a particular office or work. *The Christ* is thus the one whom God has ordained or appointed to work the works of salvation. To confess that Jesus is the Christ is to acknowledge that He is the one God sent to save the world. It is a confession about His work.

In the Old Testament God established three offices to supply leadership for His people: prophet, priest, and king. This prepared the way for Jesus to come and to combine in himself the functions of all three offices.

Jesus Is the Anointed Prophet

First Kings 19:16 speaks of Elisha's being anointed as prophet to take the place of Elijah. A prophet is simply a spokesman for someone else, one who reveals the mind of another person. Every prophet of God in some way spoke God's message to His people.

Jesus came in the office of prophet, to reveal the mind and heart of God in the highest possible way. Jesus said, "He who has seen Me has seen the Father" (John 14:9). Hebrews 1:1-3 says that God has spoken through His Son, who is "the radiance of His glory and the exact representation of His nature."

70

Jesus was anointed (for one thing) for the very purpose of preaching the gospel of the kingdom of God (Luke 4:18,43).

While we confess Jesus was truly the greatest and highest prophet, we must be careful to avoid certain extremes. This can be done if we remember three things: (1) Jesus was not the *only* revealer of God; (2) Jesus was not the *last* individual through whom revelation was given; and (3) revelation was not His principal or necessary work.

Jesus Is the Anointed Priest

The first man to be anointed priest over Israel was Aaron, along with his sons (Exod. 29:4-9). What is a priest supposed to do? Basically he is an intercessor between God and man. Specifically his work is to offer sacrifices on behalf of someone else, in order to make that person acceptable to God.

Jesus came in the office of priest, anointed to offer *Himself* as the perfect sacrifice, in order to make us acceptable to God. This was accomplished on the cross. See Hebrews 9:11-14.

A main theme of the book of Hebrews is the priesthood of Jesus Christ, especially the superiority of His priesthood over that of Aaron's family. Because they too were sinners, the Old Testament priests had to offer repeated sacrifices for themselves and for others, sacrifices that had no intrinsic power to take away guilt. (See Heb. 10:4.) But Christ is "such a high priest, holy, innocent, undefiled, separated from sinners . . . ; who does not need daily, like those high priests, to offer up sacrifices, first for His own sins, and then for the sins of the people, because this He did once for all when He offered up Himself" (Heb. 7:26,27). His sacrifice of himself on Calvary was once-for-all-time and once-for-all-sin (Heb. 9:26; 10:12). See also Hebrews 3:1; 4:14-16; 5:5-10; 8:1; 10:10-12.

There are several important Biblical words that express

Jesus' work as priest. One, of course, is *sacrifice*. Jesus is the sacrifice — the unblemished lamb — that takes away the sins of the world (Heb. 10:12; John 1:29). A sacrifice is something to which guilt is transferred, which is then offered as a substitute for the real offender. All other sacrifices are symbolic only; Jesus Christ alone is the "real thing."

Another significant word is *propitiation*. Hebrews 2:17 says Jesus became "a merciful and faithful high priest in things pertaining to God, to make propitiation for the sins of the people." Jesus died as a propitiation. See Romans 3:25; I John 2:2; 4:10.

Just what is a propitiation? Specifically it is a sacrifice that turns away wrath from the one who ought to receive it. (A gift of flowers might be a propitiation, if offered to an angry wife to help turn away her wrath.) Our sins deserve God's wrath, and God's holiness requires that this wrath be satisfied. Indeed, it is satisfied — not in us but in Christ. Our Lord turns God's wrath away from us by absorbing it in His own being. He identifies with our sins, taking them upon himself; then He takes the punishment due them. They draw the wrath of God like a magnet to our propitiation, our substitute. See II Corinthians 5:21; I Peter 2:24; Galatians 3:13; Isaiah 53:4-6.

Another word that expresses the same thing is *redemption*. To redeem means "to pay a price in order to set free." The cross is our redemption (Romans 3:24; Ephesians 1:7). From what did Christ redeem us? From the terrible debt we owe to God because of our sins: the debt of punishment, eternal punishment in Hell. We are set free from this debt, because through the cross Christ paid it for us. See Mark 10:45; I Peter 1:18,19; Galatians 3:13.

Christ's work as priest, accomplished through the cross, is His principal work. What Jesus did as sacrifice, propitiation, and Redeemer is the heart and essence of the gospel. We can be saved from eternal damnation only because our Savior has already suffered its equivalent in our place. *This is one of the most basic and most important of all Bible doctrines.*

Jesus Is the Anointed King

In Old Testament times God established the office of king over His people, and anointed various ones for this service (e.g., Saul, I Sam. 10:1; and David, I Sam. 16:13). A king is one who rules with authority and power over his subjects. Jesus came in the office of king, to be crowned King of kings and Lord of lords. See Psalm 2:1-12; John 1:49; Matthew 21:1-5; Colossians 1:15-17.

Jesus confessed His kingship when Pilate asked him, "So You are a king?" Jesus replied, "You say correctly that I am a king" (John 18:37). Paul calls this the *good confession* (I Tim. 6:13). We too make the good confession every time we acknowledge that Christ is Lord and King of our lives.

Christ's work as king is seen mainly in His battle with the devil. This part of Christ's mission is often overlooked, but Jesus did come for the very purpose of meeting and defeating His (and our) greatest enemies: the devil and death (Psa. 45:1-7; Heb. 2:14,15; Col. 2:14,15). The cross was the battleground, and the resurrection was the victory. The risen Christ is the conquering King and the Lord of all. See Colossians 1:18; Revelation 1:17,18; Romans 6:9.

At His ascension Jesus returned to Heaven in triumph and began His eternal reign. See Psalms 24:7-10; 110:1,2; Acts 2:33-36; Ephesians 1:20-23.

In summary, when we say "Jesus is the Christ," we are confessing Him as prophet — our source of truth; as priest — our sacrifice for sins; and as king — Lord of our lives.

73

JESUS IS THE SON OF GOD

How could anyone possibly do the mighty works the Bible says Jesus did? How could a mere human being accomplish such things? Well, a "mere human being" could not. That is why the Anointed One has to be more than human: He is also God. This is the meaning of the other part of Peter's confession, "Thou art . . . the Son of the living God." When we acknowledge Jesus as the Son of God, we are saying something about who He is, namely, that He is both God and man.

God the Son

Some critics object to the idea that the title "Son of God" implies that Jesus was divine. But when we examine the way it was used in Jesus' day by pagans and Jews alike, and when we see how it is used in the New Testament, it is clear that this title is a claim to deity.

For instance, John 5:17,18 records that Jesus spoke of God as "My Father." The Jews immediately sought to kill Him for blasphemy, because He was "calling God His own Father, making Himself equal with God." John 10:29-39 tells of a similar event. The Jews sought to stone Jesus because, as they said, "You, being a man, make Yourself out to be God" (v. 33). Jesus pointed out that their charge was based on His claim, "I am the Son of God" (v. 36). In other words, among the Jewish people, such a claim was definitely considered to be a claim to deity! And, it should be noted, Jesus never denied the claim or its implications! He merely said, "Here is the evidence; judge for yourselves" (John 5:31-47; 10:37,38). In fact, Jesus intensified the claim in John 5:23 when he put himself on the very same level as God the Father, saying that everyone should "honor the Son, even as [in the same way as] they honor the

Father." See Matthew 26:63-66; Luke 22:67-71.

Apart from the use of this title, Jesus is proclaimed to be God in many other ways in Scripture. Isaiah 9:6 applies to the Messiah the name "Mighty God." John 1:1 says that the personal Word who existed from all eternity and who became Jesus of Nazareth (John 1:14) "was God." As Philippians 2:6 puts it, he was existing in the form of God and had real equality with God. See Psalm 45:6; Romans 9:5; Titus 2:13.

To confess that Jesus is the Son of God is to acknowledge that He is divine, that He is *God the Son.* If He were anything less, He could not have worked the works of salvation. To deny His deity is to deny our salvation!

God in the Flesh

The remarkable thing is that God the Son appeared among us as a human being! He came not just in a temporary human form, but as a genuine, body-and-soul human being: Jesus of Nazareth (John 1:14; Philippians 2:7,8). We accept Jesus, son of Mary, as the Son of God. In other words, He had a true human nature as well as a divine nature.

We should note also that when God the Son became man, His deity or equality with God was not diminished or surrendered in any way. His divine splendor was veiled to human eyes, but He was truly God in the flesh. "In Him all the fulness of Deity dwells in bodily form" (Col. 2:9). "Veiled in flesh the Godhead see: Hail, Incarnate Deity!"

This view of the *person* of Christ is required by the Biblical teaching about the *work* of Christ. Jesus could do what He did only because He was who He was.

1. He was MAN, so He could die. Hebrews 2:9-15.
2. He was SINLESS man, so His death was not

deserved and thus could be substituted for someone else. Hebrews 4:15; 7:26-28.

3. He was the GOD-man, so His death could be substituted for more than one other person, and so He could conquer death.

CHAPTER NINE

Truth About
Conversion
God's Call

Sinners are under death's power and penalty, but Christ has conquered death. He has made salvation possible for all and desires to offer it to all. The question now is this: by what procedure can this salvation be applied to individual sinners?

This is the question of conversion. How does the unbeliever become a believer? How does the dead sinner come to life? How does the unforgiven become forgiven? What has to happen in order to bring about such a tremendous change or conversion?

Our answer to the question has two parts, because there are two elements in the process: God's call and man's response. In this chapter we are dealing only with God's call.

In John 6:44,65 Jesus shows that sinners are not predisposed to seek for salvation. God must *call* or *draw* them. (See

Rom. 8:28-30; 9:24.) But how does this take place? Because of widespread misunderstanding, it is necessary to give attention to a false view before looking at the Biblical view.

CALVINISM

One false view of God's call is found in Calvinism, a package of related doctrines taught by John Calvin in the sixteenth century (and earlier by Augustine). The Calvinistic system is usually summed up in the acrostic *T-U-L-I-P*. These letters stand for *T*otal depravity, *U*nconditional election, *L*imited atonement, *I*rresistible grace, and *P*reservation of the saints ("once saved, always saved").

We have already seen that total depravity is not a Biblical teaching. We devoted considerable space to it because of its pivotal importance in this false system. If one accepts total depravity, then the other elements in Calvinism follow logically, including the two that are related to God's call. These will be explained now (and refuted later).

Unconditional Election

As was noted earlier, the essence of total depravity is the idea of total inability, i.e., the sinner's inability to make any choice for spiritual good. Man's will is so bound by sin that his freewill ability to respond in faith to the gospel message has been destroyed. It is impossible for him to accept God's offer of salvation. According to Calvin this is a condition that afflicts every man (except Christ) because of Adam's sin.

This presents a terrible dilemma. Men need Christ's salvation but are powerless to receive it. Even if Jesus himself were to offer salvation on worldwide TV in the most forceful and persuasive way possible, no one would accept it because no one can. One may as well stand in a cemetery and offer a million dollars to anyone who will get out of his grave and come and get it.

How, then, will anyone ever be saved? The answer is simple (for the Calvinist). If man cannot choose salvation, then God will just have to choose the ones He wants to save (and let the rest stay in their sins). Why God doesn't choose everyone is not ours to ask, and the reason why He chooses this one rather than that one is just not ours to know. The belief is simply this: from all the mass of mankind, God unconditionally elects (selects, chooses) certain people to be saved.

When did God make this choice? He made it while the universe was in the planning stage. Before anything at all had been created, God had already decided which sinners He was going to save and which He was going to consign to Hell. Everything was *predestined*, unconditionally. (This is the view that most people associate with the term *predestination*.)

Irresistible Grace

This combination of total depravity and unconditional predestination prepares the way for the Calvinistic view of God's call, which is usually termed *irresistible grace*. There is, of course, an outward call that is extended to all men through the preaching of the gospel. This one can have no effect on the sinner's heart, though. So in addition to the outward call, and always in connection with it, God sends forth a special inward call to the elect only. (This "call" is not like an actual voice or actual words heard by the conscious mind.) Those chosen to receive the special call do not prepare for it, do not ask for it, do not even want it. While their wills are still bound in sin, and prior to any decision or cooperating effort on their part,

God performs a special inward operation on these selected sinners' hearts, instantaneously performing the whole work of conversion.

The Calvinist assigns this work to the Holy Spirit in particular. The Spirit supposedly descends upon the chosen one and completely changes his condition and his relation to God. The Spirit gives him a new heart (regeneration, new birth), forgiveness of sins, repentance, and faith itself — all in one package.

This call has two basic characteristics. First, it is *selective*. Only the "elect" receive it. If a person was not predestined to be saved, he is not called; he is simply left to die in his sins. Second, the call is *irresistible*. It is a supernatural act of God which the sinner cannot resist. Those who are called will respond and be saved, without fail.

Such is the view called Calvinism. We will respond to it in the next section.

THE BIBLICAL VIEW

The Calvinistic view of God's part in conversion is so closely related to the idea of total depravity that when the latter is exposed as false, the former falls with it. But even though we have already shown that total depravity is contrary to Scripture, we shall do the same for unconditional election and irresistible grace as we present the Biblical view of God's call.

Conditional Election

Many people think that predestination is an idea totally alien to Scripture, but it isn't. Paul says that God "predestined us to adoption as sons through Jesus Christ to Himself, according to the kind intention of His will" (Eph. 1:5). Also, "Whom He predestined, these He also called; and whom He called, these He also justified; and whom He justified, these He also glorified" (Rom. 8:30). See also II Thess. 2:13.

What does this mean? Are the Calvinists right after all? No, because they have misunderstood one of the most important elements in predestination, namely, the *foreknowledge* of God. From all eternity God has chosen or predestined certain ones to join the risen Christ in Heaven, but He has chosen them according to His foreknowledge of something about their lives. Romans 8:29 makes this clear: "For whom He foreknew, He also predestined to become conformed to the image of His Son." See I Peter 1:1,2.

What does God foreknow that enables Him to decide ahead of time who will be saved and who will be lost? He simply foreknows who will respond to the gospel and meet the conditions for salvation, as discussed in the next chapter. He knows this because of His ability to know everything, past, present, and future.

So there is such a thing as Biblical predestination, but it is not the same as the Calvinistic view. It differs in at least two significant ways. First, Biblical predestination is conditional, not unconditional. There are certain conditions that we must meet in order to be chosen, and we know from Scripture what these conditions are. We decide whether we will meet these conditions and be among the elect or not.

Second, contrary to Calvinism, God does not choose certain sinners and predestine them to become believers. Rather, he chooses all (foreknown) believers and predestines them to inhabit Heaven. (In Rom. 8:29, "predestined to become conformed to the image of His Son" refers to our resurrection in a glorified body just like Christ's.) God does not decide which sinners will become believers. That choice belongs to the sinner. But God does decide — has already decided — who will be in Heaven for eternity, because He has already foreseen who will accept the gospel. He knows us by name! See Luke 10:20.

The Gospel Call

Sinners' hearts *are* hardened; they are not inclined to cease their rebellion and yield to God. That is why, as Jesus says, no one can come to Him "unless the Father . . . draws him" (John 6:44). But what is the *means* by which God draws or calls sinners? Is there some unknown inner switch in our hearts that the Holy Spirit secretly flips on? No, the Bible says nothing about such an element in conversion. The means by which God calls sinners and by which the Spirit moves them to faith is simply the message of the gospel, the word of God, which has the power to cut through the armor of rebellion and plant the seeds of faith in the receptive heart. "Faith comes from hearing, and hearing by the word of Christ" (Rom. 10:17). Peter says that we are "born again not of seed which is perishable but imperishable, that is, through the living and abiding word of God" (I Pet. 1:23). See John 6:45; 12:32; 20:31; Romans 1:16; Hebrews 4:12; James 1:18.

What is the nature of this gospel call? First, it is *universal*. God does not make selections or choices. He offers salvation to all. In John 12:32 Jesus says, "And I, if I be lifted up from the earth, will draw all men to Myself." The word *draw* here is the same as in John 6:44. The message that Christ was lifted up by the cross tugs at the hearts of all who hear it. See II Peter 3:9; Revelation 22: 17.

But the call is *resistible*. It goes out to all, but all do not accept it. Sinners still have the free will either to yield to God's drawing or to resist it. As Jesus said to those who rejected Him, ". . . and you were unwilling" (Matt. 23:37). See Acts 7:51; 2:41; John 1:12.

Here, then, is the first aspect of the conversion process: God's gracious calling. The next question is, How does the sinner respond to it?

CHAPTER TEN

Truth About
Conversion
Man's Response

Man's part in the conversion process is sometimes called "the plan of salvation." This is probably too limited a connotation for such a grand expression, but we cannot tarry over semantics. Our basic concern is how a sinner reacts to God's call in order to receive the benefits of Christ's saving work.

The "plan of salvation" has been formulated in many different ways, none of which is "official." A common version is "believe, repent, be baptized, and live the Christian life." this form has serious difficulties, however; thus we are recommending a different way of putting it. Our suggested "formula" is seen in the subheadings of this chapter: By Grace, Through Faith, In Baptism, and For Good Works.

There are two basic advantages to stating the plan of salvation in this way: (1) it is more consistent with the very nature of salvation as being by grace; (2) it is based upon a single brief passage of Scripture, Ephesians 2:8-10, along with its parallel passage, Colossians 2:12.

BY GRACE

"By grace you have been saved . . . it is the gift of God" (Eph. 2:8). As the first step in the "plan," BY GRACE identifies the basis for salvation, namely, the gracious character of God and the gracious work of Christ. This helps to keep the spotlight where it belongs, even though the sinner's response is the immediate center of attention. It also helps to remind us that in whatever way we formulate the rest of the plan, *it must be consistent with grace.*

It is very important that a sinner understand the grace-character of salvation from the very beginning, so that the succeeding steps will not be misconstrued as a way of earning or deserving God's gifts. Too often this happens, and it is not the sinner's fault. Too often the plan of salvation is presented not as a way of grace, but as a law-system; and the converted sinner commences his Christian life with a salvation-by-works attitude.

When we explain to the sinner his part in conversion, we must be very careful to present it not as a law-system but as a way of grace. For instance, we should not present faith, repentance, and baptism as simply a list of commands that have to be obeyed in order to be saved (as if we were substituting a shorter law-code for a much longer one). These things should be taught not as things we *have* to do or *must* do, but as things we *can* do if we want to be saved. (This was the original idea of the plan as used by Walter Scott and others.) Let us examine ourselves: have we obscured the grace of God in our churches simply by the way we have presented the plan of salvation?

This can be done not only by the manner in which the plan is taught, but by leaving the impression that each item in the list of steps is of equal importance or that all are related to salvation in the same way. For instance, even if we say, "Here's what you *can* do to be saved: believe, repent, be baptized, and live the Christian life," we exclude grace by implying that "living the Christian life" is as important in securing salvation as is faith or baptism. Since "living the Christian life" means *good works* or obedience to God's commands, we are teaching salvation by works, not by grace.

How can this be avoided, so that grace is clarified and magnified? Perhaps by including different prepositions before the items of the plan, making it clear that they have different relationships to salvation. This is what is recommended here. "*By* grace" shows that grace is the *basis* of salvation. "*Through* faith" speaks of the *means* by which it is received. "*In* baptism" indicates the *time* when it is received. "*For* good works" makes it clear that the good works of the Christian life are not the basis or means but the *result* of being saved.

THROUGH FAITH

"By grace you have been saved through faith . . . not as a result of works" (Eph. 2:8,9). THROUGH FAITH shows the *means* by which the sinner receives the gracious gifts of God. If the sinner asks, "What can I *do* to receive salvation?" the answer is "You don't get it for anything you do; you just *receive* it in faith." (See Acts 16:30,31.)

Since salvation is by grace, it cannot be attained by any works one does. This would contradict the very essence of grace: "If it is by grace, it is no longer on the basis of works, otherwise grace is no longer grace" (Rom. 11:6). Salvation is not wages paid; it is a gift freely given. (See Rom. 4:4,5.) This is why salvation comes only through faith. Faith is not a work accomplished; it is an attitude, a state of mind, a disposition of the heart. It is submissive and receptive, and thus is consistent with grace.

So faith is the means of appropriating salvation. Some may wonder how something that appears to be so frail can be so powerful. But the power is not in the faith itself. It lies rather in the object of faith, the almighty God. We should not have faith in our faith (many people do, of course), any more than in our works. Our faith is in God and His power and His promises. Again this is why salvation by grace can only be through faith, since faith is just our acknowledgment that it is "all of God."

The essence of faith is taking God at His word. When God says something, we believe it. This means that faith gets rather specific, since God has said many things in Scripture. When God makes a statement, we believe that it is true. This is called *assent*. When God makes a promise, we believe that He can and will keep it. This is called *trust*.

Trusting God to keep His promises in Jesus Christ is *resting on grace*. See Romans 4:16-25.

We must be careful not to destroy the natural harmony between grace and faith by including works in the very definition of faith. Paul shows this is improper when he clearly sets faith and works over against each other when considered in their relation to salvation ("through faith . . . not . . . works," Ephesians 2:8,9; see Romans 3:28; 4:5). Making works a part of faith negates the whole concept of "salvation by grace through faith."

Also, we must be very careful not to destroy the freewill character of faith by making it one of the gifts of grace. Paul clearly distinguishes grace, as God's gift, from faith, as man's response ("By grace . . . through faith," Ephesians 2:8). In John 6:28,29 Jesus shows that faith is man's own decision when He calls it a "work" (in the most general sense of "something we do"). He calls it *the* work desired by God on our part.

We might also note that faith as the proper attitude toward God will always be accompanied by repentance as the proper attitude toward sin. Taking God at His word will involve a hatred of sin and a deep desire to be rid of it in our own lives. This is repentance, and thus it too is part of the attitude that receives grace. It is in a sense the underside of faith. See Luke 13:3; Acts 2:38. (Repentance does not include works themselves, in the form of an actual reformation of life. This would bring us back to a works-salvation. Repentance is the desire or disposition to change, not the actual change itself.)

IN BAPTISM

That Ephesians and Colossians (two of Paul's "prison epistles") are parallel in content is generally acknowledged. That Ephesians 2:1-11 and Colossians 2:11-13 are parallel can easily be seen by comparing the concepts contained in both, e.g., dead in sins, raised with Christ, made alive, circumcised with/without hands, God's work, through faith. But Colossians 2:12 adds one significant point not mentioned in Ephesians 2, namely, that God's work of spiritual circumcision or resurrection from spiritual death takes place IN BAPTISM: "Having been buried with Him in baptism, in which you were also raised up with Him through faith in the working of God." Grace is the basis, faith is the means, but baptism is the *time* when salvation is initially given.

The uniform teaching of Scripture is that the sinner receives the gifts of grace in Christian baptism. This is the point where he enters the saving union with Jesus Christ: "For all of you who were baptized into Christ have clothed yourselves with Christ" (Galatians 3:27). Baptism is the point of time when the guilt and penalty of sin are removed and the sinner becomes a forgiven or justified person: "Be baptized . . . for the forgiveness of your sins," says Peter (Acts 2:38). Baptism is also the specific occasion when the Holy Spirit is received into the sinner's life (Acts 2:39). This is what accomplishes regeneration or the new birth or resurrection with Christ in baptism (John 3:5; Titus 3:5; Col. 2:12). See also Acts 22:16; Romans 6:3,4; I Peter 3:21; Mark 16:16.

That these passages are referring to water baptism cannot be doubted. In the common Christian experience there is only one true baptism (Eph. 4:5). It does have two aspects, outward and inward (water and Spirit), but it is a single event. See John 3:5; Hebrews 10:22. It would be unnatural and even impossible for a Christian to read these incidental remarks about baptism in Acts or the Epistles and to exclude all thoughts of water baptism.

Many sincere people reject this clear Biblical teaching. Assuming that baptism is a work, they say salvation is through faith and not through works. This is true, but we should note that Scripture does not say we are saved *through* baptism (as a means), but *in* baptism (as the occasion). The means of receiving something is not necessarily the occasion for receiving it. The word *through* (or *by*) does not necessarily mean "as soon as," as many seem to think. God says we are saved *through faith*, but He also says we are saved *in baptism*. These two statements are perfectly consistent.

But the objection still arises, isn't baptism a work? And whether we relate it to salvation as a means or as occasion, aren't we still negating grace by making salvation depend upon a work of our own? When Martin Luther was asked this question, he responded (properly) that baptism is not *our* work, it is *God's* work. The sinner isn't doing any work in baptism. In fact, he is quite passive. He is never told to baptize himself, but always to "be baptized." The real work is being done by God (Col. 2:12, "the working of God"). God is applying the blood of Christ to the guilty soul, and bringing the dead soul to life again through the Holy Spirit. Baptism should not be included in the same category as "good works" or acts of Christian obedience. It is unique, in a category of its own.

Baptism is consistent with grace because it is in essence a *promise* of God in which we put our trust. It is not so much a command (law) as it is a promise (grace), and this is the way we should preach it. Baptism is the place where God has promised to meet the sinner and bestow upon him the gifts of salvation. Saving faith will immediately accept this promise and will rush to meet the Savior in the baptismal waters. (That faith is a prerequisite of baptism shows that infants and very young children are not intended to be baptized.)

FOR GOOD WORKS

If we are saved by grace through faith in baptism, how do

works of Christian obedience fit into the picture? Paul tells us they are the *result* of salvation: "By grace you have been saved . . . created in Christ Jesus FOR GOOD WORKS" (Eph. 2:8-10). "Created in Christ" refers to the new creation or new birth in Christian baptism (see II Cor. 5:17). God renews us so that we may be *able* to live the Christian life. (See chapter 12 in this book.)

Thus we are saved not *by* works but *for* works. Let us make sure we get our prepositions straight. Our whole understanding of salvation depends upon it!

CHAPTER ELEVEN

Truth About
Justification

We have referred to the benefits of Christ's saving work several times, but we have not discussed them in any detail. Our purpose in these last chapters is to give a more complete explanation of three of these benefits: justification, sanctification, and assurance. And what benefits they are!

In describing the sinner's predicament we have used the expression "double trouble." Our sins have affected us in two basic ways. First, sin makes us *guilty*; second, sin makes us *sick* or spiritually corrupt. One problem is a faulty *relationship*; the other is a diseased *condition*.

The salvation provided by Jesus Christ includes remedies for both these problems. One songwriter sums it up in these words: "Let the water and the blood, from Thy wounded side which flowed be of sin the double cure: save me from its guilt and power." (Or, "Save from wrath and make me pure.")

In this chapter we are specifically concerned with the solution to our problem of guilt. How does God remove our guilt and condemnation, and restore us to a right relationship with Himself and His law? The answer is seen in the Biblical doctrine of *justification*.

THE MEANING OF JUSTIFICATION

How can the sinner be justified? This is the basic question in the first few chapters of the book of Romans. God "justifies the ungodly," says Paul, not by works of law but by grace, by faith, and by the blood of Christ (Rom. 3:20,24,28; 4:5; 5:9).

Exactly what happens when God justifies us? What does it mean to be a justified person? The term basically has to do with righteousness. (The root word means "righteous, just.") Some have interpreted justification to mean a state of actual righteousness or holiness. "To justify," they say, means "to *make* righteous, to *make* holy and pure." This is the way the Roman Catholic Church teaches it. The decrees of the Council of Trent (VI:7) specify that justification includes "sanctification and renewal of the inward man . . . whereby man . . . becomes just." God makes us just, so that we "are just, receiving justice within us." Others have followed Catholicism here, including several of the better-known cults.

This understanding of justification misses the point, however. "To justify" does not mean "to make righteous" but "to *declare* righteous, to pronounce or count righteous, to treat as righteous." This point is clearly seen in Luke 7:29, which says literally that the people "justified God." Obviously this means they *declared* Him to be righteous, not made Him righteous.

What this means is that justification is not a change in our condition, not an inner transformation of our sin-corrupted nature. It is an objective, external change in our relationship to God and His law. It is basically the same as forgiveness or remission of sins. See Romans 4:6-8.

Justification is a *legal* concept and must be understood in the context of a court of law. Guilt itself is a legal term, i.e., a wrong relationship to law; therefore justification as its remedy must be seen in the same light. Precisely speaking, "to justify" is the exact opposite of "to condemn." Judges, says Deuteronomy 25:1, are supposed to "justify the righteous and condemn the wicked." Romans 8:33,34 asks, "God is the one who justifies; who is the one who condemns?" See Proverbs 17:15; Matthew 12:37.

The best way to remember what justification means is to picture a judge in a courtroom bringing his gavel down and declaring "NOT GUILTY!" To be more precise, the judge justifies us by declaring, "NO PENALTY FOR YOU!" Even though we are guilty, God the Judge treats us as if we were not guilty (Rom. 4:5); though we deserve a penalty, He does not assign one.

The bottom line of justification is this: if we are declared "not guilty," then *no sentence is pronounced against us.* We are free from all penalty, punishment, condemnation, and wrath. "There is therefore now no condemnation" (Rom. 8:1). Though we are sinners, God treats us just as if we had never sinned, or more precisely, just as if we had already paid our entire penalty. ("I am *justified*" means God treats me *just [as] if I'd* already paid my penalty.)

Obviously there is no benefit more urgently needed by sinners, and none for which believers should be more joyfully grateful.

THE BASIS OF JUSTIFICATION

Our next subject is the *basis* of justification. When a judge declares "Not guilty!" or "No penalty for you!", on what basis does he reach that decision? What considerations warrant such a verdict of acquittal? He does not act without a good reason.

One possible basis for such a decision is the person's actual innocence. If the evidence shows he has committed no crime, then the judge *must* justify him on the basis of his *works*. This is how one could possibly be justified before God by law or works of law if he were one hundred percent good or innocent. The basis of his justification would be his own righteousness or good works.

God does not have this option in our case, though, because we have all sinned. Thus it is impossible for anyone to be justified on the basis of works. See Romans 3:19,20. Our works only show us to be guilty; our works deserve only punishment. How then can God look directly at guilty sinners and say, "Not guilty"? Is it possible that God can "justify the ungodly"? See Romans 4:5.

Yes, praise God, it is possible, but only on one basis: the blood of Christ (Rom. 5:9). God can declare us "not guilty" and treat us as if we had never sinned only because Jesus has already stepped in and taken our place; He was counted guilty for us and received the punishment due to us. On the cross He placed himself between us and the consuming fire of God's wrath. His death has satisfied the justice of God and the requirements of His law.

When we come to Jesus Christ we come to the one who has already paid our debt. Thus when God sees us holding on to Christ He says, "Oh, you're with Jesus! In that case we can let you go, since He has already 'served your sentence' for you. Case dismissed!" This is why "there is therefore now no condemnation for those who are in Christ Jesus" (Rom. 8:1).

This is how "the blood of Jesus His Son cleanses us from all sin" (I John 1:7). Our sins are washed away (Acts 22:16), washed off the books and no longer held against us. When we are "in Christ Jesus" — under His blood — God in a sense does not see our sins; they are blotted out from His sight.

Many will remember the red-cellophane illustration. Picture a sheet of white paper on which the outline of a human figure is drawn with black ink, then defaced with scrawls of red ink. When a piece of clear red cellophane or plastic is placed over the drawing, the scarlet defilement is "blotted out" from our eyes. In just this way we are "justified by his blood" in God's sight.

The basis of our being counted righteous, then, is the actual righteousness of Christ, not our own righteousness (good works). *Righteousness* means satisfaction of the requirements of the law. This can be achieved in two ways, either by obeying its commands or by suffering its penalty. Jesus did both, but it is the latter that justifies us. His "one act of righteousness" (Rom. 5:18) — His atoning death — is counted for us, setting us free from the law's penalty.

This is the "righteousness of God" which is the essence of the gospel message and the basis for our hope (Rom. 1:17; 3:21,22; 10:3; II Cor. 5:21; Phil. 3:9). It is the "robe of righteousness" that God gives us to cover our own filthy rags (Isa. 61:10; 64:6). As the song says, "My hope is built on nothing less than Jesus' blood and [Jesus'] righteousness"!

This is what it means to be "justified as a gift by His grace through the redemption which is in Christ Jesus" (Rom. 3:24). Here the distinction between law and grace is most clear. Under law one could be justified only by his own perfect works — only if he is one hundred percent good. But under grace we are justified on the basis of Jesus' work, which makes us one hundred percent forgiven.

THE MEANS OF JUSTIFICATION

What must the sinner do in order to be justified? What is the *means* of receiving justification? As we saw in the preceding chapter, in the system of grace the only means of receiving justification is by faith in Jesus Christ. "For we maintain," says Paul, "that a man is justified by faith apart from works of the law" (Rom. 3:28). See Romans 5:1; Galatians 2:16. Paul is emphatic about faith being the means of justification, and he is just as emphatic in denying that we are justified by works. In Romans 3:28 the preposition *apart from* says that we are justified by faith apart from a consideration of our works, good or bad. See Romans 4:6-8.

Does this mean that as long as we have faith, then it doesn't matter whether we obey or not? Absolutely not! The Bible is very clear that the faith that justifies is a faith *that works* — through love (Gal. 5:6). Faith necessarily leads us to obey. We are created in Jesus Christ "for good works" (Eph. 2:10).

James 2:24 even says that "a man is justified by works, and not by faith alone." The difference between Paul and James is a matter of emphasis. Paul is speaking precisely: the only thing *directly* related to justification is faith. Of course, this faith is always accompanied by obedience. See Romans 6:1-19. James simply makes the same point more emphatically by saying that in a sense we are justified by works; i.e., works are *indirectly* related to justification, since the faith that justifies is a faith that works. Otherwise how can anyone know that faith exists? (James 2:18).

We can summarize it thus: we are not justified by faith *and* works (Paul). Nor are we justified by faith *without* works (James). Rather we are justified by a faith *that* works (Paul and James).

THE TIME OF JUSTIFICATION

As we noted earlier, to say that we are justified *by* faith does not mean we are justified *as soon as* we have faith. Means and time are two different things. God has specified the time when we begin to be justified, namely, in Christian baptism, where we meet Jesus and come under His blood through faith. We put on Christ (our robe of righteousness) like a garment in baptism through faith (Gal. 3:26,27). We are baptized unto the remission of sins (Acts 2:38). We are buried with Christ, into His death, *in baptism* (Col. 2:12; Rom. 6:4-6).

But the main point of the Bible's emphasis on justification by faith is not the way we initially receive it, but the way we keep it. We continue to be justified from the time of baptism, on through the Christian life, as long as we continue *truly to trust in Jesus' blood.* In baptism we become justified persons; through faith we continue in a state of being justified, a state of grace (Rom. 5:1,2). See Romans 8:1; Ephesians 3:17; I Peter 1:5.

Some people still think of baptism as the point where we receive forgiveness for past sins only. This way of speaking obscures the fact that God's forgiving work in baptism has continuing results. It is not just a matter of washing away past sins, but of receiving a robe of righteousness that continues to cover us after baptism (Gal. 3:27). Not only sins, but *persons* are forgiven in baptism; and the forgiveness or justification is constant and continuous, even though we sin. Apostasy or falling away from grace is possible, but one sin or even a dozen sins do not necessarily constitute apostasy. (Where faith abides, every sin will be followed by sincere repentance, of course.) Apostasy comes when we lose our faith, when we no longer trust in Jesus, when we do not have confidence in His forgiveness, or when we no longer consider Him Lord and try to obey Him.

The relevant questions have been asked by a songwriter: "Are you washed in the blood of the Lamb? Are you fully *trusting* in his grace *this hour*? Do you rest *each moment* in the crucified?" Then you are free — free from guilt, free from condemnation, free from worry about Hell, free to concentrate on serving God and obeying Him from love alone!

CHAPTER TWELVE

Truth About
Sanctification

Let us remember that sin causes two basic problems: guilt and sickness, and that salvation includes remedies for both. As we have just seen, justification removes our guilt. But if that were all there is to salvation, we would still be weak and helpless and held down by the chains of sin. We would be unable to make much headway in conquering our sinful habits, tendencies, and desires.

But maybe that doesn't matter. After all, if we are justified by grace through faith, are works even necessary? Do we still *have* to obey God's commands? Does it really matter whether we keep on sinning or not? We can understand how some may be prompted to ask such questions, since the gospel of grace is so amazing, even radical, when compared with ordinary concepts. See Romans 6:1: "Are we to continue in sin that grace might increase?"

But of course it matters! How could anyone even think otherwise? (Rom. 6:2). This is why God has made provision not only to remove our guilt, but also to restore our sin-weakened natures to a state of spiritual life and health. This is the second part of the "double cure," in which God destroys sin's power over us and makes us pure.

The process by which God accomplishes this is sometimes called *sanctification*. This is what we will be discussing in this chapter.

THE MEANING OF SANCTIFICATION

To *sanctify* means to make holy; *sanctification* means holiness. A sanctified person, a holy person, and a saint are all the same. These are all just different ways of translating the same Greek and Hebrew words, so we should not look for a difference in the meaning of the English words.

Especially from the way the Old Testament uses the term, we can see that sanctification or holiness has two basic aspects. First there is ontological holiness, which is the state of being separated or set apart from the ordinary. This corresponds to God's holiness in the sense of transcendence; He is separated from or different from creation itself. The second aspect is ethical holiness, which has to do with separation from sin. This corresponds to God's holiness in the sense of moral purity and righteousness.

A Christian is sanctified in both senses. There is first the *initial* sanctification, when we are separated or set apart by the blood of Christ from our old way of life and from "this present evil age" (Gal. 1:4). This is an *event* that occurs at

Christian baptism, when the blood of Christ is applied (I Cor. 6:11; Heb. 10:29; 13:12). This transfers us from the domain of darkness into the kingdom of Christ (Col. 1:13). We transcend the old creation to become a part of the new (II Cor. 5:17). This is an accomplished fact. Those who have been thus sanctified or set apart are called saints (I Cor. 1:2).

This one-time event is not the only sense in which we are sanctified. There is also *progressive* sanctification, which is the process of growing in grace and knowledge, overcoming sin, and developing pure conduct and a holy character. This is like God's holiness in the sense of His separation from sin; only with God it has always been the case, whereas we have to work our way into it. Sanctification in this sense means becoming more and more like God in righteousness and holiness of truth (Eph. 4:22-24). "Like the Holy One who called you, be holy yourselves also in all your behavior; because it is written, 'You shall be holy, for I am holy' " (I Pet. 1:15,16). See II Peter 1:4; 3:18.

Some groups, particularly those of the Wesleyan tradition, speak of "entire sanctification." They believe that by a "second work of grace" God bestows upon the Christian a state of moral perfection in this life. This view has little to support it in Scripture, however, and all experience seems to belie it. Sanctification continues as a growth process throughout the Christian life. We strive toward complete holiness (I Thess. 5:23; Matt. 5:48), but expect to achieve it only after death. (See Heb. 12:23, "the spirits of righteous men made perfect.")

THE POSSIBILITY OF SANCTIFICATION

The model for holiness after which we try to pattern our

lives is God's Own holy character (I Pet. 1:15,16). We know the nature of His holiness only through the revealed words of Scripture. In this sense we are sanctified by the word of God. See John 17:17; Acts 20:32; I Peter 2:2.

Just knowing from Scripture what we ought to do, however, does not mean that we are going to be able actually to do it. Considering the sinner's state of spiritual weakness, we recognize that knowledge alone is not sufficient to produce holiness. Even when we are touched and motivated by the word of God to forsake wickedness, we realize that from our own resources we do not have the possibility and power to overcome the hated sin and do good. See Romans 7:14-24.

But this is precisely what God has provided as part of the benefits of Christ's saving work, namely, the possibility and power for living a sanctified life. In this section we will discuss what God has done to make sanctification possible.

Before a person is saved, it is impossible for him to do works which are truly good, i.e., good on the inside as well as the outside. The sinner is spiritually dead (Eph. 2:1) and thus separated from God. In this state of unbelief he cannot do works that please God. "Without faith it is impossible to please Him" (Heb. 11:6). Until the tree itself has been changed, it will continue to produce evil fruit (Matt. 7:16-18; 12:33-35).

But in conversion God *changes* us so that we are free from the power of sin and able to attain holiness. This change is called regeneration or rebirth (Titus 3:5; John 3:5); re-creation (Eph. 2:10; II Cor. 5:17); and resurrection from the dead (Eph. 2:5,6; Col. 2:12,13). It is a change worked upon our hearts by the Holy Spirit. It is a change in our actual *condition*, in contrast with justification (a change in *relationship*). Both regeneration and initial sanctification occur at the same time, but it is important to see that there is a distinction between them.

This change is not comparable to the Calvinistic idea of irresistible grace. According to the latter, the Spirit enters and changes the sinner's heart prior to desire or faith. But in Biblical regeneration, the sinner is brought to faith and to the desire for change by the Word of God, after which he yields himself to the changing power of the Spirit of God. This "working of God" takes place in Christian baptism, where the Holy Spirit is given and the sinner is raised to new life. See Acts 2:38; Colossians 2:12; John 3:5; Titus 3:5.

Exactly how the Spirit works and the exact nature of the change are not explained in Scripture. The important thing, though, is not the *nature* of regeneration, but the *result* of it. It is plain that the purpose of the inward change is to make it possible for us to be holy, to live the Christian life. Ezekiel 36:26,27 prophesies, "I will give you a new heart and put a new spirit within you. . . . And I will put My Spirit within you and cause you to walk in My statutes." Ephesians 2:10 is quite specific: "For we are His workmanship, created in Christ Jesus for good works." The very purpose of the inward, re-creating work of the Holy Spirit is to equip us *for good works.* This provides the possibility for sanctification.

THE POWER FOR SANCTIFICATION

When the Holy Spirit is given to us in Christian baptism, the immediate result is new life. The long-range result is that the Spirit continues to dwell in our very bodies and lives. Paul says the Christian's body is a "temple of the Holy Spirit who is in you" (I Cor. 6:19). Jesus promised that the Spirit would be present in believers like a refreshing fountain: "He who believes in Me, as the Scripture said, 'From his innermost being shall flow rivers of living water.' But this He spoke of the Spirit, whom those who believed in Him were to receive . . . " (John 7:38,39). See Romans 8:9-11.

Why does the Holy Spirit come to dwell within us? To *sanctify* us, to make us holy. He does this not by giving us more knowledge, either through new revelation or some kind of mystical "guidance." (He gives us knowledge through the Bible.) Rather, the Spirit sanctifies us by giving us *power.* By being present within us in a special way, He is a ready source of spiritual power and strength. We work with Him, but we cannot be sanctified without Him.

In the early days of Christianity the Holy Spirit gave miraculous power to certain ones in the church. These miraculous spiritual gifts had a special purpose and filled a particular need that existed only in the early decades of the Christian era, namely, before the New Testament had been completed and circulated to the churches (see I Cor. 13:8-13). We should not expect to receive this kind of power from the Spirit today.

The power which the Spirit does give us, though, is much more significant and useful for Christian living. He provides us with *moral* power, spiritual strength, power to resist temptation, overcome sin, and be good. He strengthens our wills to fight against sin and to work out this aspect of our salvation, namely, our sanctification. Paul's prayer is that God "would grant you, according to the riches of His glory, to be strengthened with power through His Spirit in the inner man" (Eph. 3:16). You *can* "work out your salvation" because "it is God who is at work in you, both to will and to work for His good pleasure" (Phil. 2:12,13). See Romans 8:12-14; I John 4:4; I Corinthians 10:13.

The Holy Spirit is present with us to give us power, but He can do this only if we consciously and deliberately commit ourselves to fight sin and seek holiness. If we do this, He will help us; He will give us inner strength to be good. We must not rely merely upon our own resources and will power, though. We must rely instead upon the Spirit's power; we must trust God's promise to supply strength through the Spirit. Ephesians 3:16 is a good model to use in praying for this inner strength.

THE MOTIVE FOR SANCTIFICATION

Some have the mistaken idea that salvation by grace relieves us of the *obligation* to obey God's commands. Nothing could be further from the truth. The obligation to obey God is grounded in the fact of creation (Psa. 24:1,2), and nothing can ever change it. Being saved by grace has no effect whatsoever on this obligation. Freedom from law does not mean freedom from obedience. Under grace we are free from law as a way of salvation, but not as a standard and a rule of obedience.

Salvation by grace does involve a significant change in our *motivation* for obedience, however. We must be very careful not to confuse objective obligation (why we *ought* to do something) with subjective motivation (why we actually *do* it). Though the former never changes, the latter changes tremendously when we come under grace.

When a person is trying to be saved by law (i.e., lawkeeping), his works are the basis and means of his salvation. Hence he will be motivated to obey by a desire to escape Hell and reach Heaven — period. But under grace escaping Hell and reaching Heaven are gifts received by faith, not by works. Hence these should no longer be our motives for obedience. We try to live the Christian life not from fear of punishment or desire for reward. Knowing that we are justified by faith frees us from these inferior motives.

What is our motivation for fighting sin and trying to be good? It is the strongest motive of all: *grateful love*. If we truly love God (and how can we help but love Him after all He has done for us? I John 4:18,19) — if we truly love God, we will want to please Him by doing His will. "If you love me, you will keep my commandments," says our Lord (John 14:15). Faith works; it works through love (Gal. 5:6).

CHAPTER THIRTEEN

Truth About
Assurance

"How can I be sure?"

From a practical standpoint, this is *the* question. Our greatest conscious need is for a feeling of confidence regarding our present acceptance by God and our future participation in glory. We need "blessed assurance," the assurance of salvation.

What is assurance? Is it possible to have assurance? If so, what is the basis for it? These are the questions we will try to answer in this final chapter of *His Truth*.

There are several approaches to the question of assurance, some of them contrary to the teaching of Scripture. Here we will examine two false views before explaining the Biblical view.

"ONCE SAVED, ALWAYS SAVED"

The two most popular erroneous concepts of assurance are at opposite ends of the spectrum. One is the common idea, "Once saved, always saved"; the other is the view that assurance is impossible.

The "once saved, always saved" position is often called "eternal security." The idea is that once one becomes a true believer, it is impossible for him to lose his faith (permanently, at least) and therefore impossible for him to lose his salvation. From the moment one initially receives the benefits of Christ's redemption, he is eternally secure. He need not worry about ever falling away from grace. God will preserve him in faith forever.

This view is an integral part of the total system of Calvinism. The "P" in the T-U-L-I-P acrostic stands for "perseverance (or preservation) of the saints." It follows logically upon the ideas of total depravity, unconditional election, and irresistible grace. Even prior to creation God unconditionally decides which totally-depraved persons He will save; then at the appointed time He irresistibly calls them and gives them the gift of faith. Since God is in sovereign control from beginning to end, He will infallibly see to it that every believer maintains his faith until the end. So says the thoroughgoing Calvinist.

We should remember that Calvinism denies the freewill nature of faith. "Once saved, always saved" is just another aspect of this denial. In this system one cannot believe and accept salvation of his own free will, nor can he cease to believe and cast salvation aside of his own free will. Religious groups that are fully Calvinistic (e.g., most Bible-believing Presbyterians) accept the system in its logical totality. Other groups (e.g., some but not all Baptists) inconsistently hold to the doctrine of eternal security but reject the rest of the Calvinistic system, which serves as its foundation.

We must reject the view of "once saved, always saved" as being contrary to Biblical teaching. Certainly God will not cast *us* aside (John 10:28,29; Rom. 8:31-39), but it is quite possible for us to cast *Him* aside. The Bible clearly teaches the conditional nature of salvation. Both receiving it and keeping it are conditioned on our freewill surrender to Christ as Lord. *"If* you abide in Me, . . . *if* you keep my commandments," says Jesus (John 15:7-10), you will be all right. But *"if* anyone does not abide in Me, he is thrown away as a branch, and dries up; and they gather them, and cast them into the fire, and they are burned" (John 15:6). Or as Paul says (Col. 1:23), *"If* indeed you continue in the faith firmly established and steadfast, and not moved away from the hope of the gospel," you will be saved. But, he says (Rom. 11:20-22), *if* you do not continue in God's kindness, you will not be spared; you will be cut off.

That one can fall from grace is the underlying assumption of the whole book of Hebrews. The very theme of this book is the possibility, danger, and foolishness of abandoning one's faith in Christ. Apparently a group of Jewish Christians were having doubts about their conversion to Christianity and were considering a rejection of Christ and a return to pre-Christian Judaism. The letter to the Hebrews was written to dissuade them from this apostasy.

For instance, Hebrews 6:4,5 speaks of those "who have once been enlightened and have tasted of the heavenly gift and have been made partakers of the Holy Spirit, and have tasted the good word of God and the powers of the age to come." Obviously this description can refer only to those who are truly Christians. But, says Hebrews 6:6, if these "have fallen away, it is impossible to renew them again to repentance" as long as they continue to recrucify Jesus Christ. Obviously this refers to a real falling away from grace. See also Hebrews 2:1-3; 3:6-14; 4:1,11; 10:26-39; 12:25.

Thus we conclude that "once saved, always saved" is not the Biblical view of assurance.

"TRYING HARD, NEVER SURE"

The other extreme to be avoided is the one that might be summarized as "trying hard, never sure." Those who take this position deny the possibility of assurance altogether. Even though we work hard at being Christians, we can never be sure of our good standing with God, they say.

Some people go to this extreme when they reject the eternal security idea. They mistakenly equate the unconditional assurance of "once saved, always saved" with assurance as such. Thus when they reject the former, they cast aside all assurance along with it.

The most common reason for uncertainty about personal salvation, though, is a faulty understanding of grace. There are many Christians who, in one way or another, still think that salvation is by works, i.e., by being *good enough.* Anyone who thinks this way, and at the same time knows that he is an unworthy sinner, is bound to be plagued with doubt and worry and despair. He knows he is not good enough. The best he can hope for is to die in church or while praying his daily prayer for forgiveness. At the same time those who do claim assurance he condemns for being proud and boastful, as if they were claiming to be good enough to be saved. But salvation comes from being forgiven, not by being good.

The "trying hard, never sure" approach to assurance has as little Biblical support as "once saved, always saved." Both extremes must be rejected. Then what does the Bible say?

BIBLICAL ASSURANCE

The Biblical approach to assurance is well summed up in the words of I Peter 1:5 — we are "protected by the power of God through faith." This emphasizes both God's faithfulness and the Christian's faith as essential elements in assurance.

"Protected by the Power of God"

"Protected by the power of God" stresses God's faithfulness. We can be sure that He will never forsake us or cast us aside. (See Heb. 10:23.) We can be sure that He will provide all the resources we need to protect us from our enemies. (See John 10:28,29; Rom. 8:31-39; I Cor. 10:13; II Thess. 3:3; I John 4:4.) These resources include the indwelling Holy Spirit, the Bible, prayer, and the church with its fellowship and its shepherds.

The greatest resource of all is God's own faithful and unfailing love. This love is the firm basis for our assurance, according to Paul's teaching in Romans 5:1-11. In this passage Paul shows that salvation involves two basic transitions. The first transition is from *wrath to grace*; the second is from *grace to glory*. The transition from wrath to grace is by far the most difficult, the most extreme, and the most unlikely. But the love of God found a way to make it possible. How can we doubt, then, that His love will take us through the next transition, which is so much less radical by comparison?

It is vital that we see the progression of Paul's thought in this passage. This is the sum of it: the love of God provided the ultimate gift for us while we were His *enemies*, so it certainly will not fail us now that we are His *friends*. What did God do for us while we were His unreconciled, sinful, helpless enemies? No less than give His own Son to suffer in our place (Rom. 5:5-8). But if God's love would do that for us while we were His enemies, we can have every assurance that He will do even more for us now that we are justified and reconciled (Rom. 5:9,10).

Will not God save those at *peace* with Him, if He went to the extremity of dying for His *enemies*? Will not His love suffice to make the less radical change that remains? Can God's love for His friends be less than His love for those who hate Him? If the love of God could span the vast chasm between wrath and grace ("in which we stand," v. 2), how "much more" can this same love span the lesser chasm between grace and glory! This "much more" of God's love is the basis for our assurance.

"Through Faith"

First Peter 1:5 says we are protected by God's power "through faith." This simple expression tells us two things about assurance. First, it shows that assurance is not absolute and unconditional. Certainly God's love is unconditional, but whether we allow ourselves to experience His love is conditioned upon our faith. As long as we freely continue to trust God's gracious promises, He will keep us in His grace. If we cease to trust, then by our own decision we cut ourselves off from Him.

The fact that God protects us "through faith" thus shows that assurance is conditional. As long as we have sincere faith in God's promises in Jesus Christ, we can be sure of our present relationship with God. But there is always the possibility that sometime in the future we may lose our faith and fall from grace (Gal. 5:4). We assume, though, that every sincere Christian will do his very best to maintain his trust in Jesus Christ.

That God's protection is ours "through faith" leads to a second conclusion, namely, that our assurance of salvation is not conditioned upon works. As we have already seen, we are justified by faith apart from works measured by law (Rom. 3:28). *Knowing that we are justified by faith is the real key to assurance.*

To be *justified* means to be at peace with God (Rom. 5:1), to be free from condemnation (Rom. 8:1). To be justified *by faith* means that this peace and freedom are not conditioned on how good we are (i.e., works), but on our continuing trust in the all-sufficient blood of Christ. Returning for a moment to Paul's discussion of the two transitions in Romans 5:1-11, we see that our part in the first transition is summed up in the word *faith.* We have crossed the chasm from wrath to grace by faith (Rom. 5:2), not by works. And just as surely as we did not span this first and forbidding chasm by any works of our own, neither will the second chasm be spanned by our works. God spans them both by His grace, and we cling to His grace by our faith.

To put it another way, our sense of assurance derives from knowing we are *justified* by the blood of Christ, not from our having achieved a certain level of *sanctification.* The question is not "How *good* am I?" but "How *forgiven* am I?" and we know that we have been one hundred percent forgiven, ever since our baptism, because of Christ.

This assurance of our present relationship to God through

Jesus Christ gives us the "hope of glory" (Rom. 5:2; Col. 1:27). *Hope* is assurance concerning the future; it is a confident expectation of something good. In common usage *hope* is often no more than a wish, but not so in Scripture. Biblical hope is *hope* because it refers to the *future*, not because it is uncertain. See Romans 8:24,25. And we who are presently justified by the blood of Christ through faith have this hope, this confident expectation of sharing in His glory throughout eternity.

"And every one who has this hope fixed on Him purifies himself, just as He is pure" (John 3:3).